analogies ARQUITECTURE

animal

ANALOGIES BETWEEN THE ANIMAL WORLD AND CONTEMPORARY ARCHITECTURE

Alejandro Bahamón
Patricia Pérez

Parramón
Architecture and Design

Editorial direction:
María Fernanda Canal
Editor:
Alejandro Bahamón
Coordination:
Ana Cañizares
Theoretical framework:
Patricia Pérez Rumpler
Jimena Arango
Research:
Alex Campello
Correction:
Isabel Núñez
Art direction:
Mídori
Graphic design:
Soti Mas-Bagà and Pilar Cano
Illustration:
Elisa Riera
Production director:
Rafael Marfil
Production:
Manel Sánchez

Editorial project:
latinta
www.latinta.net

Published by Parramón Ediciones, S.A.
Ronda de Sant Pere, 5, 4ª planta
08010 Barcelona (España)
Empresa del Grupo Editorial Norma de América Latina

www.parramon.com

Prepress:
PACMER, S.A

ISBN: 978-84-342-3515-1
Printed in Spain

Introduction

Patricia Pérez

The analysis of the morphology of animals for the purpose of aiding in the design of utensils, structures, and machines has been a feature of human life from mankind's most primitive stages right up to the complex social structures of today. The use of animal forms in contemporary architecture—whether to endow a project with symbolism, seek functional solutions, or simply for esthetic reasons—has become a recognized, indeed commonplace, practice. Architects of the stature of Renzo Piano, Norman Foster, and Frank Gehry, for example, have all opted to use animal forms in some of their most recent buildings.

This book does not attempt to assemble generic examples of zoomorphism in contemporary architecture, but rather seeks to focus on specific analogies with animal strategies to protect the body from toxic substances, radiation, vibrations, impacts, humidity, and all other types of negative external influences, without blocking contact between the exterior and the interior. These strategies can be divided into various categories. First, animals are equipped with innate defensive elements that shield the flesh throbbing within. This capacity is known in biological terms as "armoring." Apart from these defense mechanisms, animal species base their possibilities of survival on attack, flight, concealment, or camouflage (passing unnoticed is an inoffensive, effective way of staying alive). Of special interest for our purposes is the skill exhibited by some animals in the construction of their own protective architecture or, to put it another way, the configuration of their own spaces to further their everyday activities.

The term "animal architecture" was coined in 1974 by the Nobel Prize winner Karl von Frisch (1886–1982), who demonstrated the capacity of some not particularly complex animals to create sophisticated constructions with a noteworthy degree of technological expertise. Human beings are not the only ones capable of creating new environments or modifying the world around them. Furthermore, as O. T. Mason points out in his article "Technogeography, or the Relation of the Earth to the Industries of Mankind," we have undoubtedly copied techniques from animals in order to apply them in various ways and make them more complex and efficient. Technological limitations obliged primitive hunter-gatherers to maintain a close relationship with other creatures, and many experts therefore consider it highly plausible that human beings borrowed inventions from the animals with which they lived.

Man's capacity to accumulate experience and transmit information from one generation to the next has combined with his constructive imagination to allow him to surpass his mentors in the art of building and develop his own techniques to an extraordinary degree. This supremacy and specialization acquired by humans with respect to animals has meant that the former rarely pay any more attention to the apparently precarious and primitive constructions of the latter. This attitude, bordering on arrogance, finds its most perverse expression in the existence and proliferation of the classic dog kennel. Nevertheless, the observation of animals' building activities can, even today, be enormously enriching for architects, as this book hopes to demonstrate.

Without a doubt, elements of the wasp nest, mousehole, bear den, mole burrow, rabbit warren, etc., have persisted in the shelters in which we live. Just as the observation of children never ceases to surprise and enrich adults, the study of animal structures represents a leap back in time to the first stages of architecture, which laid the foundations for the work being done today. A reexamination of these structures—however simple they may appear—can provide information of the utmost value to the development of contemporary architecture. Similarly, the reincorporation of these forms—so original, essential, and pure, but also practical, logical, and sustainable—can offer an alternative to the often untenable sophistication all around us.

Finally, it should be pointed out that this book not only compares and contrasts techniques and materials used in animal constructions with examples of human architecture, but also includes information about animal behavior related to habitation. The common expression "abandoning the nest" demonstrates the existence of analogies between human and animal behavior in terms of living space. Rediscovering conduct that we consider human in animals is, apart from its undeniable comic value, a way of remembering where we came from. The curiosities from the animal world that resonate in our own environment include monkeys preparing a bed every night, swallows enjoying a second residence during the coldest months of the year, tree frogs building a kindergarten to protect their tadpoles, and cuckoos squatting in other birds' nests.

In contrast, there are many other strategies that are exclusive to the animal world that can open up new approaches and act, at the very the least, as a stimulus for projecting new forms of habitation. The shedding of the outer skin experienced by animals such as the snake and the lizard should not be dismissed from an architectural viewpoint, for it works against deterioration and enhances maintenance by enabling the organism to grow, by helping mend wounds, and by eliminating unwelcome external parasites. Meanwhile, monk parakeets have evolved a very specific mechanism to allow them to conserve a degree of intimacy in collective homes—they live in nests containing up to eighty individuals, but each pair of birds has its own private entrance.

To finish on a humorous note, the great bowerbird (*Chlamydera nuchalis*) builds not only nests but also extraordinary courtship arbors, designed to attract females during the mating season. If this strategy should also prove to facilitate fluid communications between humans, we should not rule out the idea of inserting similar "lonely-hearts architecture" into the landscape. The latter examples, along with the others presented below, serve as a reminder that nature not only provides us with materials, but also often sets out guidelines for subsequent interventions.

The book's structure is organized around four chapters. The first refers to anatomical structures, incorporated into the animal itself; the next two chapters explore constructive structures artificially created by animals, while the final one deals with preexisting structures that are appropriated by certain animals.

Anatomical Structures
Animal Constructive Structures
Social Animal Constructive Structures
Temporary Constructive Structures

Skin Hair Armor Shell

Anatomical Structures

The tegumentary system, also known as the outer cover, surrounds an animal's body and allows the organism to come into contact with the environment. In architecture, the term "skin" is often used to define the perimeter wrapped around an interior to separate it from the exterior. Surely architecture is our third skin, after clothing. Similarly, the terms "membrane" to describe the enclosures that enhance the fluid exchange between "inside" and "outside" and "protective shell" to evoke impregnability now form part of today's architectural vocabulary. Nature has created a diversity of forms proper to the tegumentary system to protect animals from external attacks of all kinds. There are many similarities between architecture and the tegumentary system, with the common basis of a passive but efficient defense of an interior without any renunciation of vital exchanges of information and of thermal, aqueous, and gaseous material.

The bodies of mammals are covered with tegumentary formations known as hair, which grows out of bulbs embedded in the epidermis. Every hair has the ability to stand upright through the action of a small erector muscle. Hair has a protective function, as it regulates body temperature and enhances the evaporation of sweat, as well as acting as a sensory organ.

On birds, feathers not only favor propulsion but also perform an isolating function. Plumage allows air to accumulate in the host of spaces left free by the spongy mass, thus creating a veritable tissue of feathers. Active life subjects feathers to constant wear and tear, so they grow and are periodically replaced by other similar ones in a process known as the molt.

In order to protect themselves from any harm, hedgehogs roll themselves up so that their most vulnerable areas are sheltered inside the "ball" and confront their enemy with strong quills that emerge out of their coat. A porcupine, swinging its tail, can insert its quills (up to 12 inches [30 cm] long) into the body of aggressors. The quills normally remain close to its body, but when the animal is excited, they stand up and move vigorously and threateningly, making a distinctive dry sound by knocking against each other. The effectiveness of the porcupine's defense lies in the fact that the strong adhesive tips of the quills are much more resistant than their growing, supportive bases.

A tortoise's body is protected by an armor shell made up of various bony sections overlaid by hard, horny layers. The part

Scales Shell Snail Hermit Crab

covering its back is called the carapace, while the protection of the underside is known as the plastron, and the two are joined together at the edges, thereby enclosing the soft areas of its body in a sturdy sheath. The head, the limbs, and the tail can be withdrawn to provide the animal with total protection in the case of danger. A tortoise's shell grows, adding new material to the interstices of its shields and thereby increasing its volumes.

Anteaters have the upper part of their body and the outer surface of their paws covered by large, overlapping plates that are sharp and horny. This arrangement turns these animals into veritable living armored vehicles. In the case of the armadillos, the structure of their horny mosaic is polygonal in form and consists of plates juxtaposed in lines running across their body. In the mid-dorsal section, these plates acquire sufficient mobility to allow the body to both roll up and stretch up.

Some crustaceans and arachnids exhibit skin hardened by a cladding of chitin that can also be considered an armor shell. There are soft joints between the various sections that prevent the body from becoming too rigid, bestowing mobility on the hard pieces of the shell while also benefiting from their protection.

Fishes' bodies are covered with bony, overlapping scales that shield their skin, which is lubricated by an array of mucous glands. The bodies of reptiles are covered by a tegument hardened by keratin, and in the case of crocodiles this is further strengthened by bony plates. Snakes shed their skin to allow their body to grow normally inside their stiff sheath of scales.

The skin surrounding most mollusks is so thin that it usually exudes a covering known as a mantle in the dorsal section. The secretion of the mantle produces shells designed to protect the body. These come in different shapes, from the double shell of clams to the helicoid of the snail.

The hermit crab is also equipped with a shell that defends the rear of its body. However, this structure is not developed by the crab's body but is taken from a dead mollusk: this crustacean's strategy consists of occupying other shells. In order to make its body fit inside the shell, it curls up its abdomen, while its pincers enable it to block the entrance. The hermit crab is obliged to change its shell as it grows.

Shell

This station is situated between a kindergarten and a school on the outskirts of the town of Casar de Cáceres, in Extremadura, Spain, and so it is constantly being passed through not only by bus passengers, but also by children. The architect wanted to evoke the imagination of infants and connect the structure with their dream world. He sought a design that would succeed in satisfying the station's functional requirements and came up with wavy sheets of white concrete, inspired by the analogy of seashells. The result was a distinctive landmark that oversees the to-and-fro of children as well as the arrival and departure of passengers, who reach the station after traveling past the vaulted buildings characteristic of the streets in the town center. The station's entrance, echoing this local architecture, is formed by the structure's smallest sheet, which protects passengers as they move toward the central area. The two sheets constituting the body of the station serve as both the floor and the roof, curling inside each other to maximize the space. The larger sheet covers the parking lot for buses as well as providing an exit, while the underground part of the structure contains a bar and storage space, and supplies a more complete view of the complex, by which one is better able to appreciate the sensation of movement running through it.

Site Plan

Client

Department of Public Works, Junta de Extremadura

Type of Project

Bus station

Location

Casar de Cáceres, Extremadura, Spain

Total Surface Area

15,285 square feet (1,420 m2)

Completion Date

2003

Photos ©

Hisao Suzuki

Casar de Cáceres, Extremadura, Spain

Casar de Cáceres Bus Station

Justo García Rubio

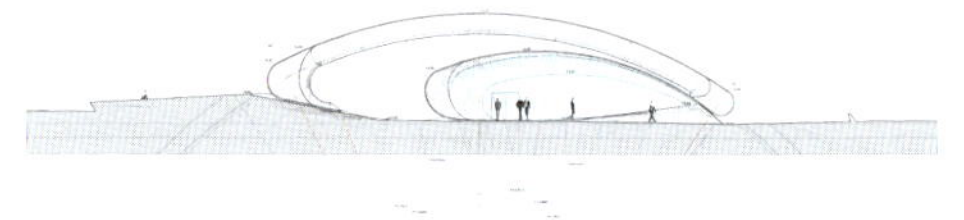

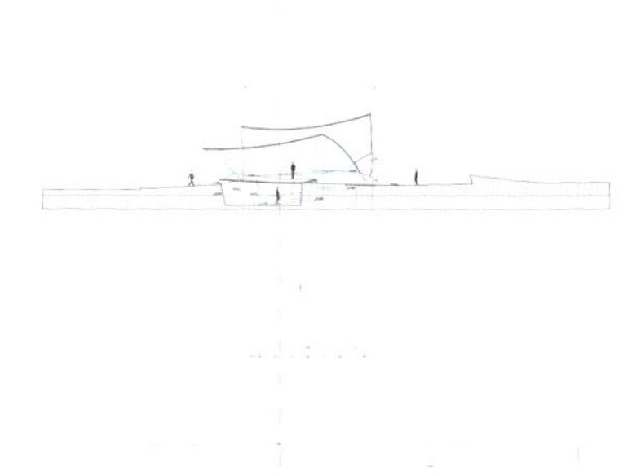

Geometric Studies of the General Composition

The concrete sheets used in the station give rise to an interesting transformation of the structure into a sculpture and vice versa. The form of the main sheet is a hyperbola 111.5 feet (34 m) long and 46 feet (14 m) wide, relatively small in comparison with the general structure which creates the sensation of a central arch and generates an aerodynamic effect when the wind crosses the arch. This architecture, based on the continuous structures of armor shells, has a great geometric impact, apart from reducing the costs of construction, because it succeeds in configuring the various architectural elements, the roof, the interior space, and the façade with a single material and a single form.

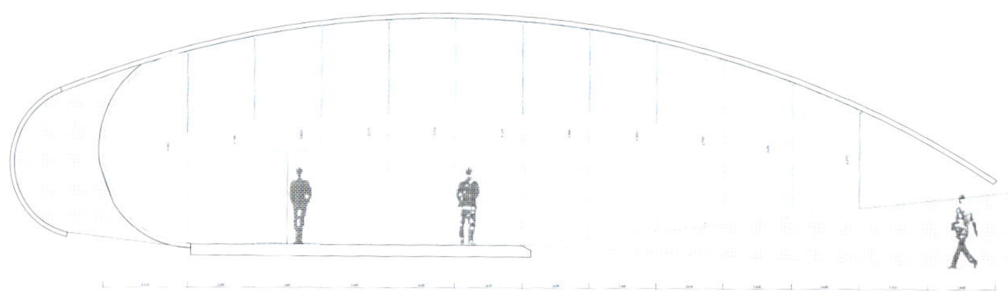

Platform Elevation

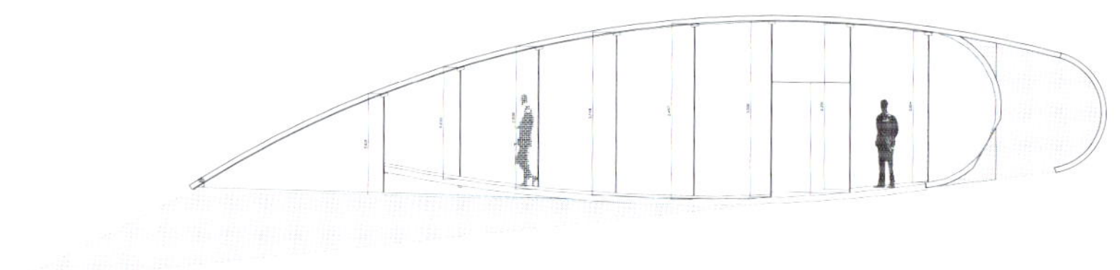

Street Elevation

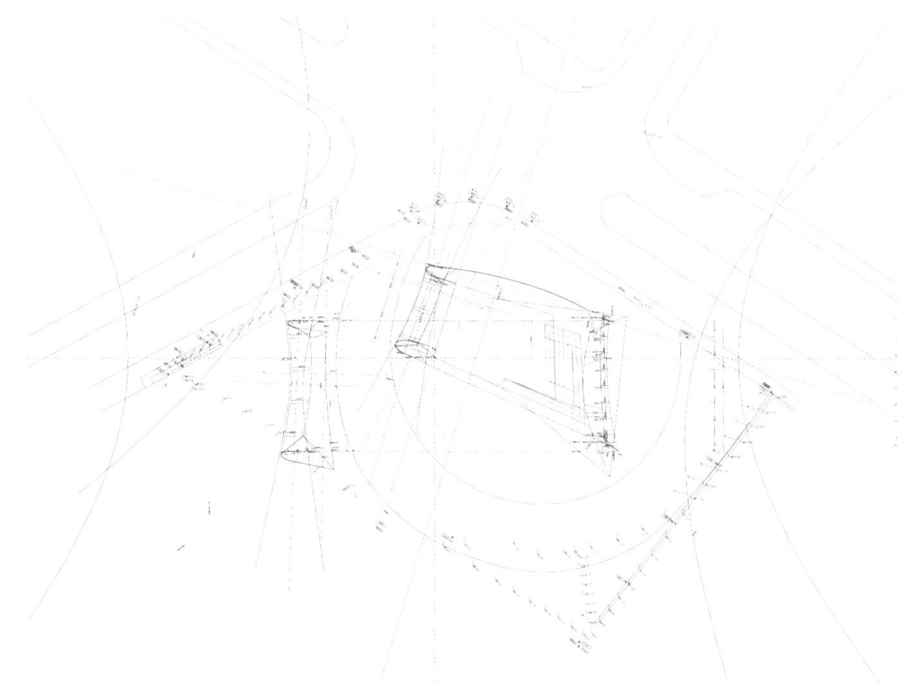

Geometric Plan

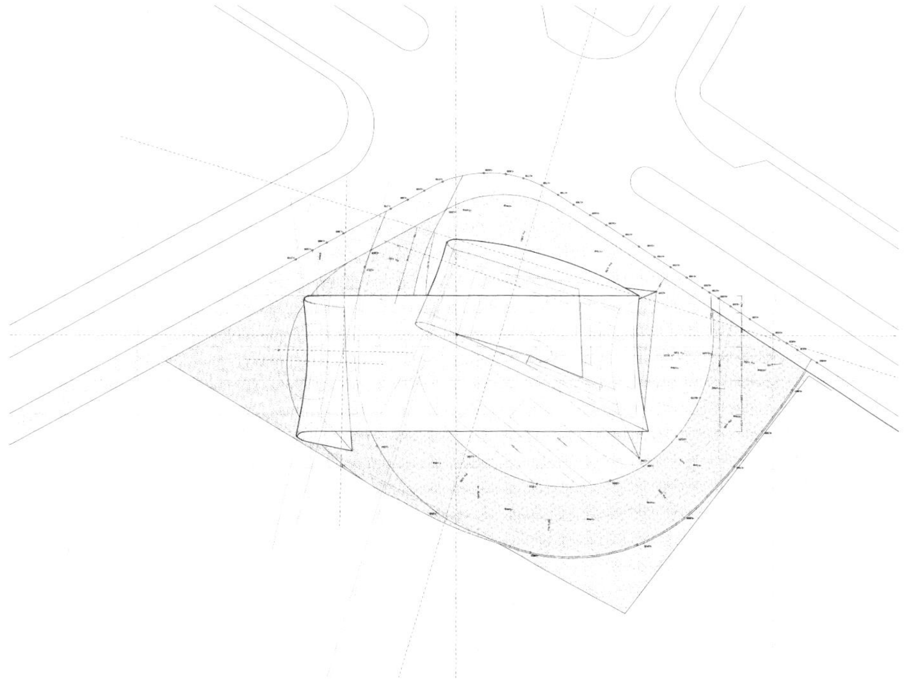

Plan of the Roofs

Geometry of the Main Sheet

Detail of the Supports of the Plank Molds

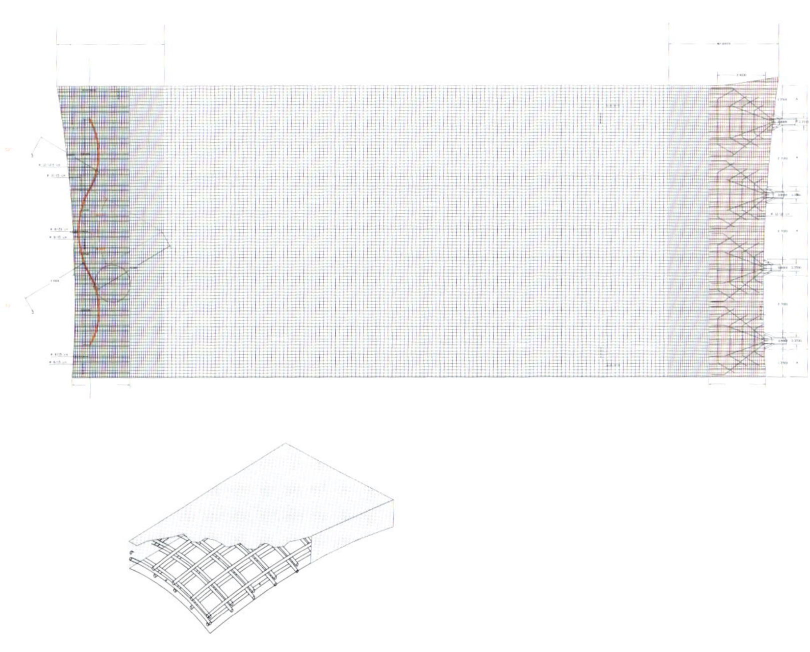

Structure of the Main Sheet

The two materials used to make the structure—white concrete for the sheets and gray concrete for the floor (which also acts as a support)—reinforce the distinction between the underground architecture and that of the upper sheets. The elevated structure of the sheets is perceived as two separate, light objects that give the impression of moving from one side to the other with the wind. In the underground area, the floor is built in such a way that the ground seems to rise up to act as a support, mark frontiers, or become a curved wall that highlights the route of the buses, while avoiding any disruption of the spatial relationship with the park situated behind the station.

Snail

The Science Museum in Glasgow, Scotland, is one of the city's most important buildings; it has breathed new life into the once-dilapidated dockland area. The museum has three main buildings—a science center, an IMAX theater, and a rotating tower 161 feet (127 m) high, with a 360-degree view of the city—but all three merge into a single entity. The science center and the theater are linked by a glass entrance and a smooth tissue that serves as a roof, while a discovery tunnel connects the science center with the tower. The three buildings can be considered exhibitions in their own right, as their services, structures, and finishing are innovative, experimental, and scientific. The building's external shells are clad with titanium, aluminum, glass, and granite. This was the first time that titanium was used to cover a building in the United Kingdom, and it adds a distinctive touch to the structure. The materials used on the inside are exposed concrete, natural wood, steel, and glass. The half-moon shape of the science center constitutes the main building in the complex; its titanium curve on the south side protects the exhibition galleries from direct sunlight, in contrast with the front area, where sunshine is allowed to pour inside. The IMAX theater, the first of its kind in Scotland, has a seating capacity of 370. The titanium shell protects the auditorium, while the front part of the building is wrapped in a glass membrane.

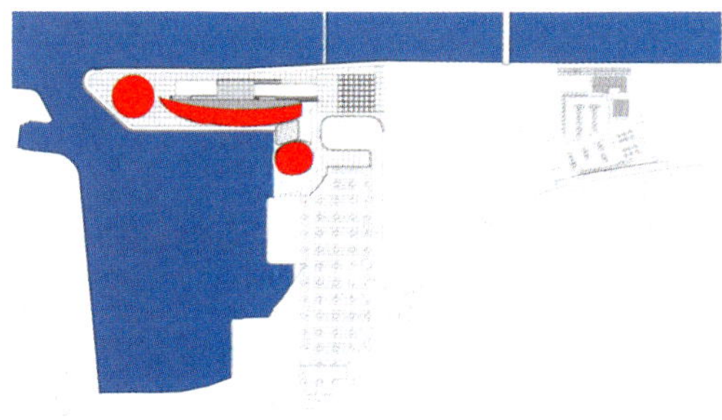

Site Plan

Client
Glasgow City Council

Type of Project
Science center

Location
Glasgow, Scotland

Total Surface Area
161,459 square feet (15,000 m²)

Completion Date
2001

Photos ©
Zooey Braun | Artur

Glasgow, Scotland

Glasgow Science Museum

Building Design Partnership

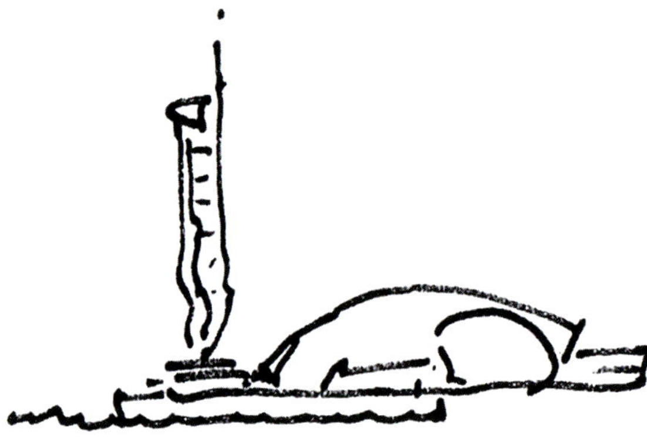

Preliminary Sketch

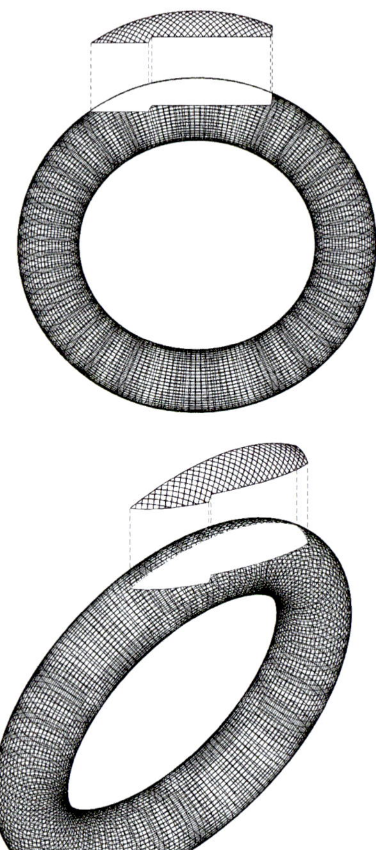

Geometric Study of the Volume

Concern about the structure's self-sufficiency and other environmental issues particularly influenced the initial design with respect to placement, mass, engineering, materials, and energy sources. So, the science center takes advantage of natural light in the spaces between the galleries, thereby reducing the costs of artificial lighting. Similarly, the natural ventilation, the high thermal mass, and the location next to the river were all exploited in order to save energy. The shell covering the southern part of the science center reflects the path of the sun and is designed as a mold capable of integrating all types of systems for absorbing energy in order to conserve and recycle it for internal exhibitions or scientific purposes. Other technical resources—such as photovoltaic cells, solar panels, and state-of-the-art glass—will later be added to the structure's skin.

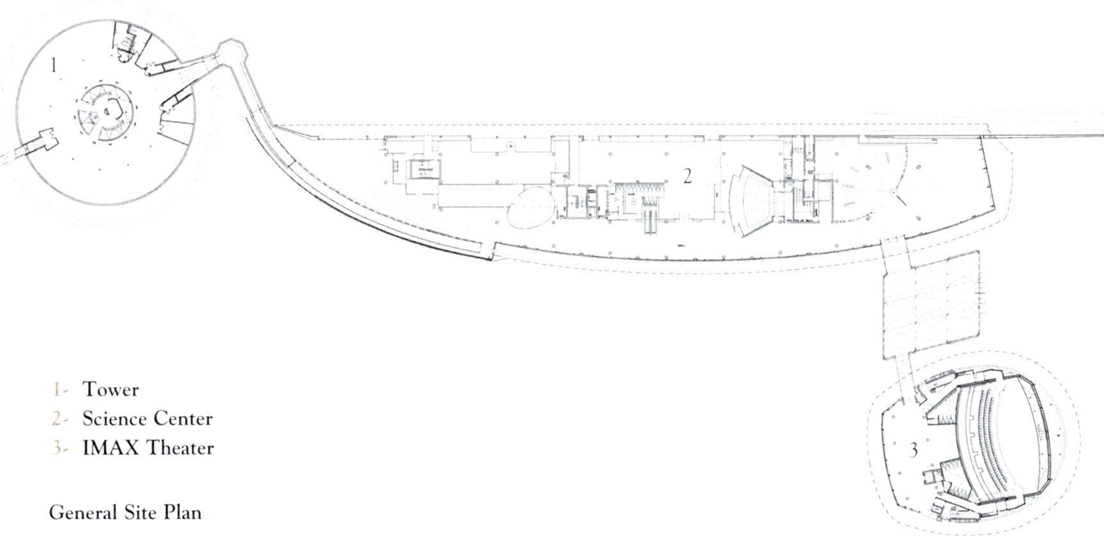

General Site Plan

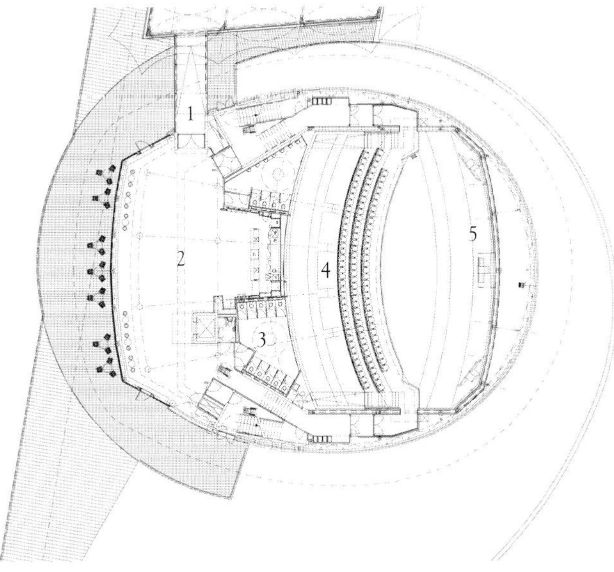

1- Entrance
2- Foyer
3- Restrooms
4- Seating
5- Screen

IMAX Theater, Ground Floor

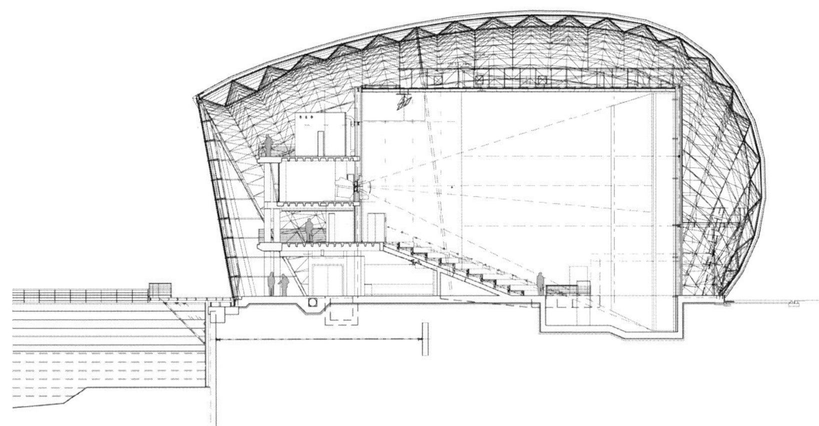

IMAX Theater, Cross Section

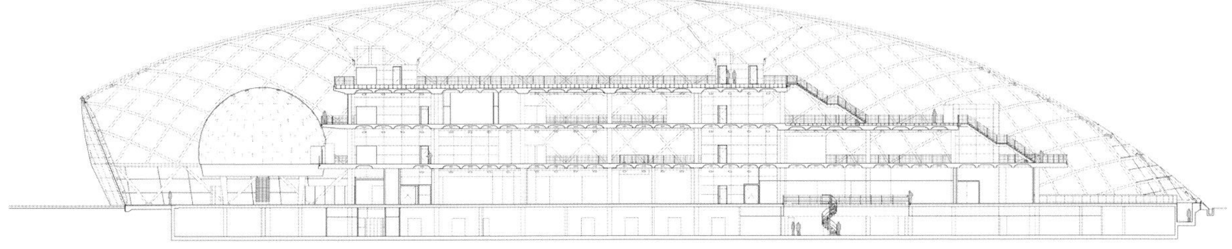

Science Center, Longitudinal Section

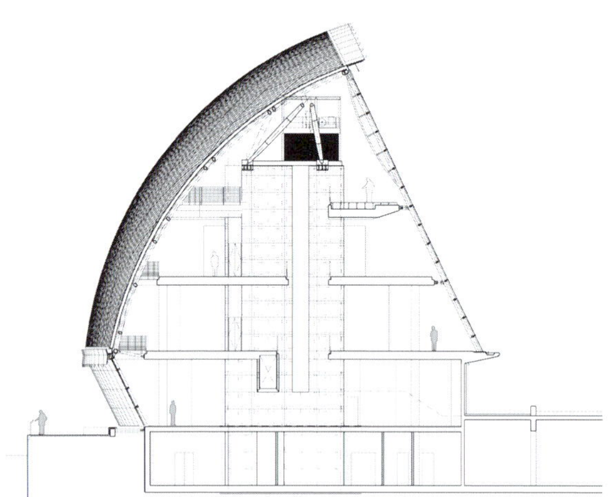

Science Center, Cross Section

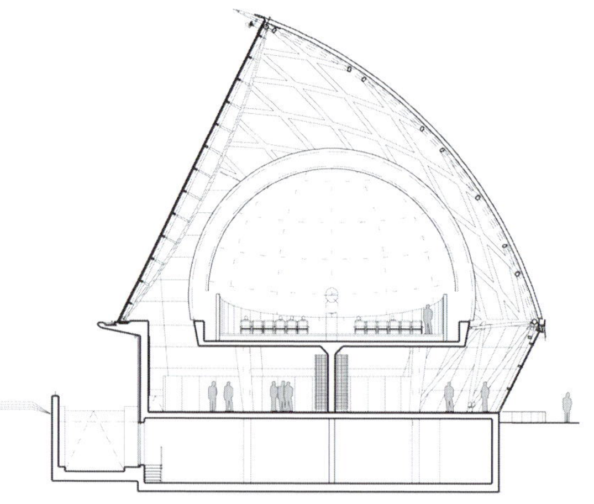

Science Center, Cross Section

GSC Clyde Explorer

Snail

Torrevieja is a town on the Mediterranean coast of southern Spain with a popular spa. It has a population of around 60,000, although this figure rises tenfold in summer because of the visitors attracted by its idyllic beaches and the surrounding landscape of mountains and lakes. The emblematic pink lakes, which change color in daylight because of their high concentration of phyto-plankton, bacteria, and salt, add to the charm of the area. Thanks to its well-known therapeutic properties the mud from these lakes is used in various spas in the region. The aim of the park was specifically to provide access to these benefits without radically altering the surroundings (in contrast to the general procedure in recent years). The project was based on a structure akin to a spa, gently unfolding through the sand dunes to preserve the harmony with the natural environment of the beach and the lakes. The structure is buried in the sand like a giant shell, and this form is echoed in the three buildings that will eventually house a res-taurant, an information center, and open-air baths in the second construction phase.

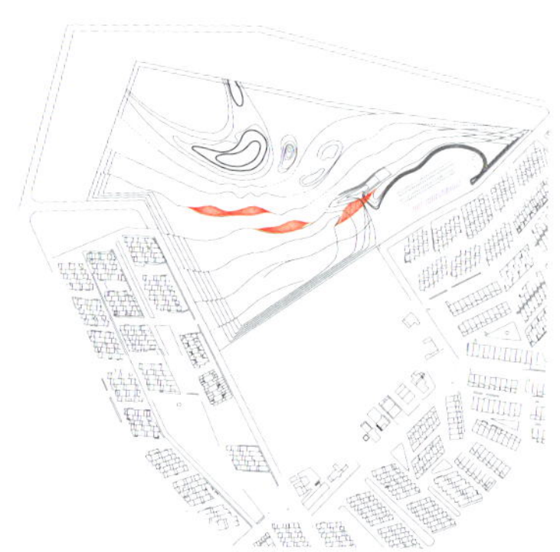
Site Plan

Client
Torrevieja Town Hall

Type of Project
Spa center

Location
Torrevieja, Alicante, Spain

Total Surface Area
13,400 square feet (1,245 m²)

Completion Date
2005

Renders ©
Daniel Suárez Zamora

Torrevieja, Alicante, Spain

Torrevieja Park

Toyo Ito & Associates, Architects

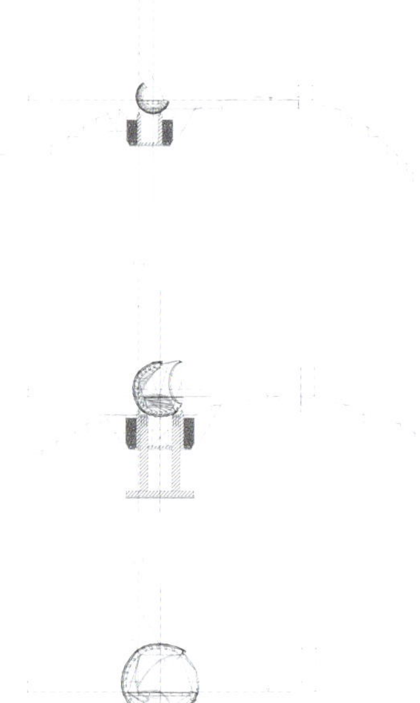

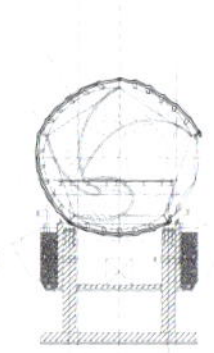

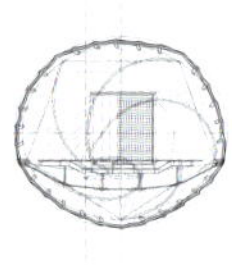

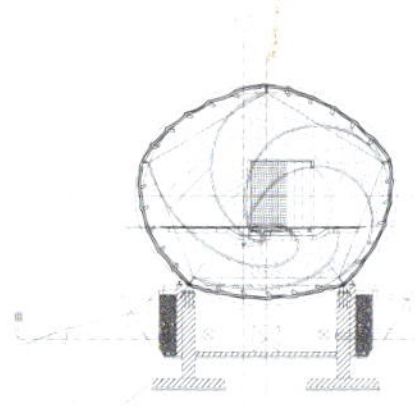

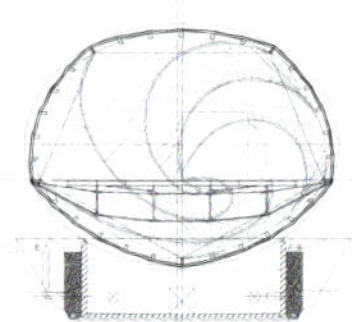

Development of the Volume in Section

Although at first sight the structure appears complicated, its design is in fact based on a very simple system. The planes in the form of a snail were generated by Bézier curves, which bestow continuity on the landscape, and the radius of the ellipse is derived from the length of the main axis. Five steel bars 2.36 inches (60 mm) in diameter, joined to wooden beams 14.8 to 16.5 feet (4.5 to 5 m) long, are interwoven into the structure in a spiral to create the form of a snail. Some outdoor elements are covered with plywood sheets, a feature that endows the structure with the effect of a skeleton, bringing it closer to the animal's organic form. The entresols, which are also supported by the spiral armature, connect the steel bars and give the building greater rigidity and stability.

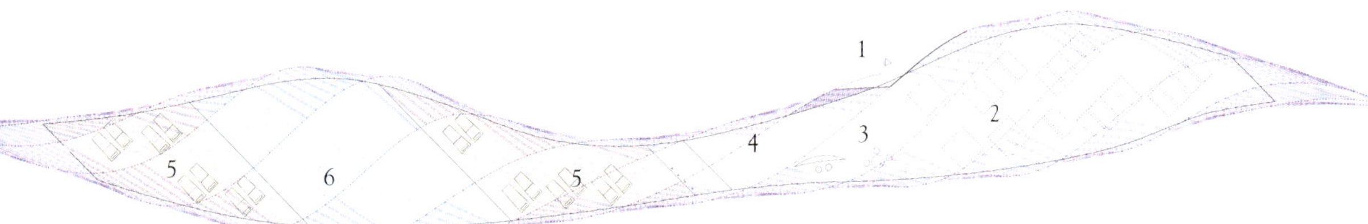

Plan, Spa Building

1- Entrance
2- Hot-Sand Bath
3- Reception
4- Showers
5- Relaxation Areas
6- Hot-Water Bath

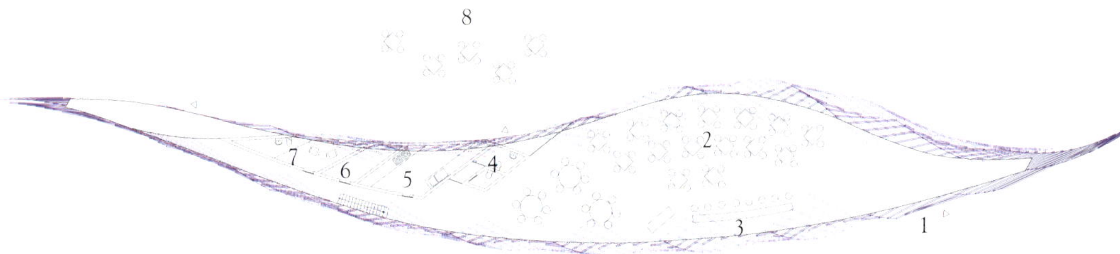

Plan, Restaurant Building

1- Entrance
2- Dining Room
3- Bar
4- Restrooms
5- Kitchen
6- Storage Area
7- Office
8- Outdoor Eating Area

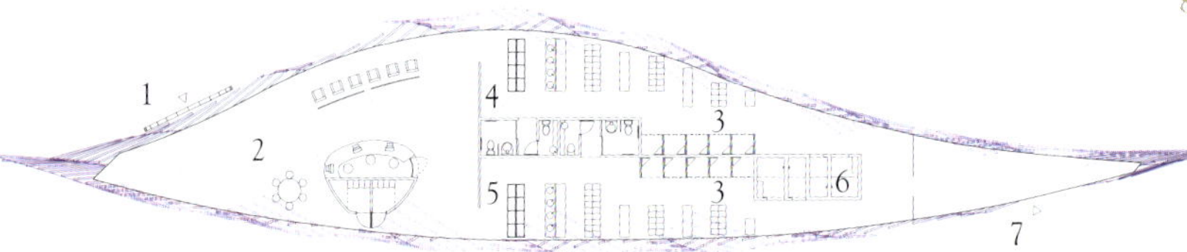

Plan, Information Building

1- Entrance
2- Reception
3- Cabins
4- Men's Room
5- Women's Room
6- Showers
7- Secondary Entrance

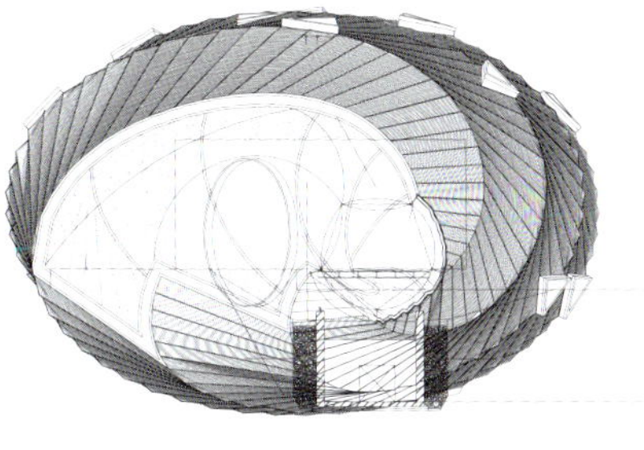

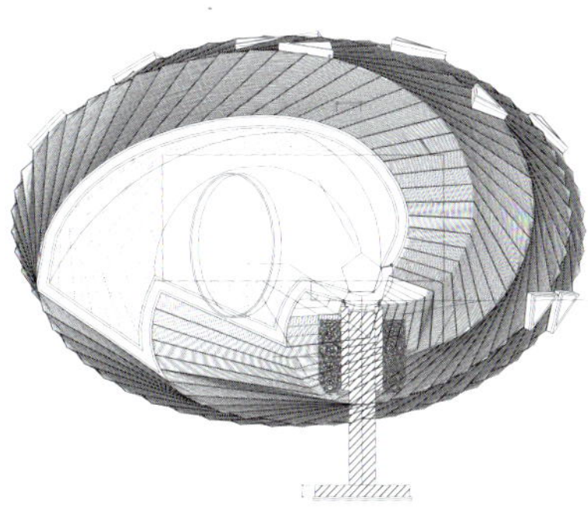

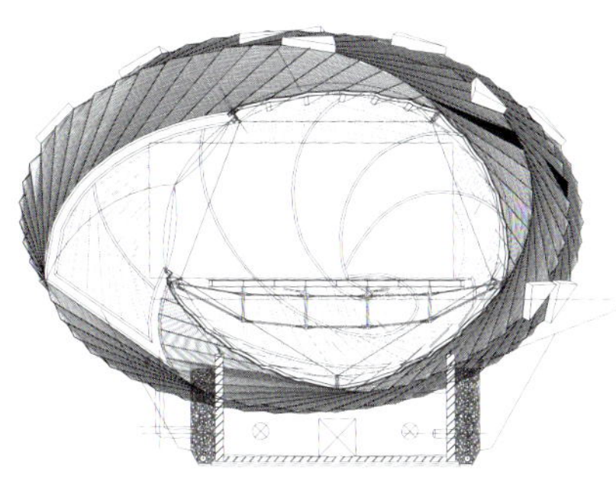

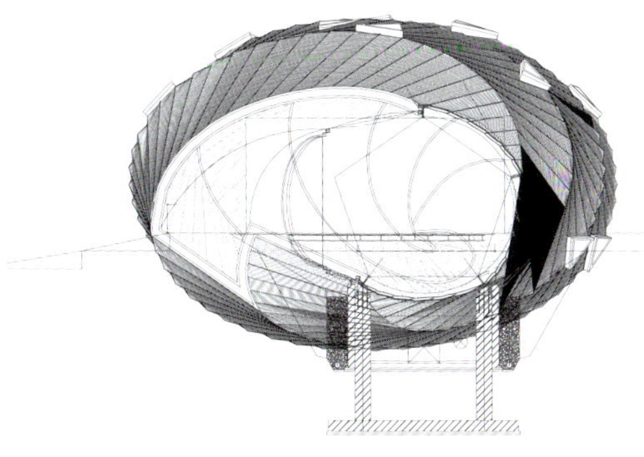

Cross Sections

Armor Shell

Brno-Tuřany International Airport is situated close to a freeway on the southeastern plain of Brno, the second-most-important city in the Czech Republic. The main aim of this project was the creation of a new departures terminal, intended to improve both the airport's operating conditions for workers and the quality of service for customers, while also helping to establish the airport as part of the European international network, in accordance with the new regulations for the Schengen states. (The Schengen Agreement of 1985, pertaining primarily to border control issues, has been signed by thirty, mostly western, European countries.) The project also sought to boost the development of the southern region of Moravia by consolidating commercial activities associated with tourism and air travel. The building is distinguished by the compact, aerodynamic form that protects its fragile interior, inspired by the armor shell of various animals. The structure, totally exposed to view (both inside and out), resembles a skeleton covered by a steel skin. The façade required a long phase of design and technological development to optimize its resistance to atmospheric conditions. To achieve this, a special hexagonal model was created to satisfy the structure's technical requirements. Although the building opened only recently, it has already become a center of attention and has consolidated the city's status as the "gateway to the world and the country," as well as stimulating the general development of the area.

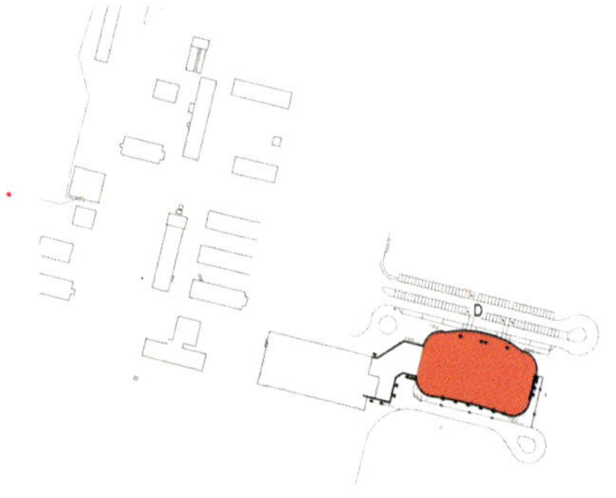

Site Plan

Client
Kaláb and Pr mysl Veselý

Type of Project
Airport terminal

Location
Brno, Czech Republic

Total Surface Area
43,055 square feet (4,000 m^2)

Completion Date
2006

Photos ©
Petr Parolek, Tomás Ludvík

Brno, Czech Republic

Brno Airport–
Departures Terminal

Petr Parolek

Preliminary Sketch

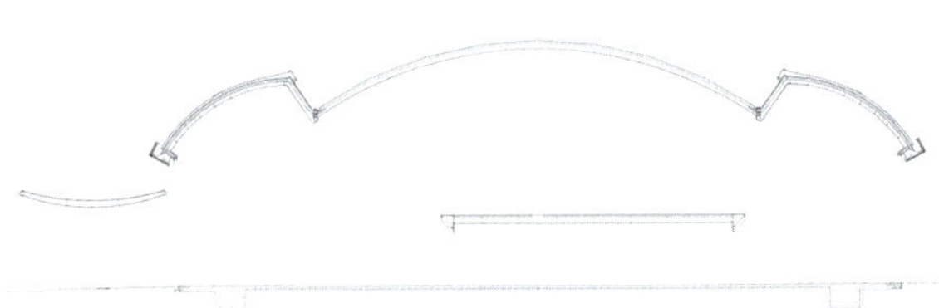

Schematic Section

The structure is supported by six steel vaults, integrated into a formal curvilinear concept. Light enters from the northeast side, through various asymmetrical naves in the form of glass arches set into the roof. The external part of the armature is divided in the third sector of the structure to form the side bodies of the main corridor. The building is notable for its round armature, which leads to a significant saving of energy, and for its capacity to integrate natural ventilation by means of light shafts. The main arches on the external façade dominate both sides of the terminal, while the north face is endowed with arches in the form of wings that protect passengers at the entrance. The south entrance is covered by a modern system of solar blinds that reduce the ventilation costs, while also revealing a superb panoramic view of the surrounding landscape.

The rounded forms of the clear, simple architecture of the exterior not only evoke the structures of an armor shell, but also follow the principles of aerodynamics applied to airplanes and other means of transport.

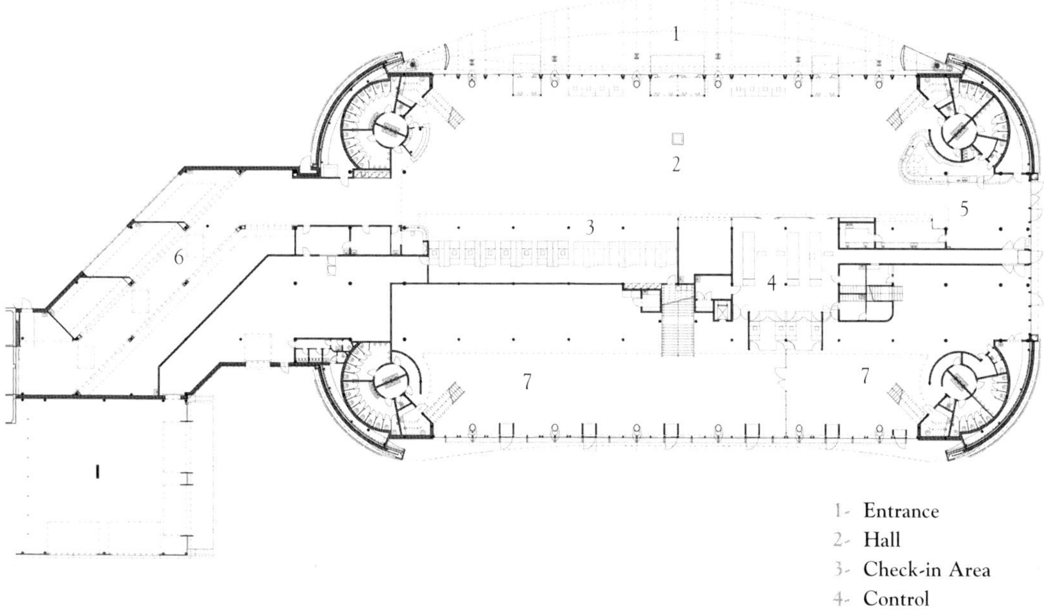

1- Entrance
2- Hall
3- Check-in Area
4- Control
5- Cafeteria
6- Walkway
7- Waiting Rooms

Ground Floor

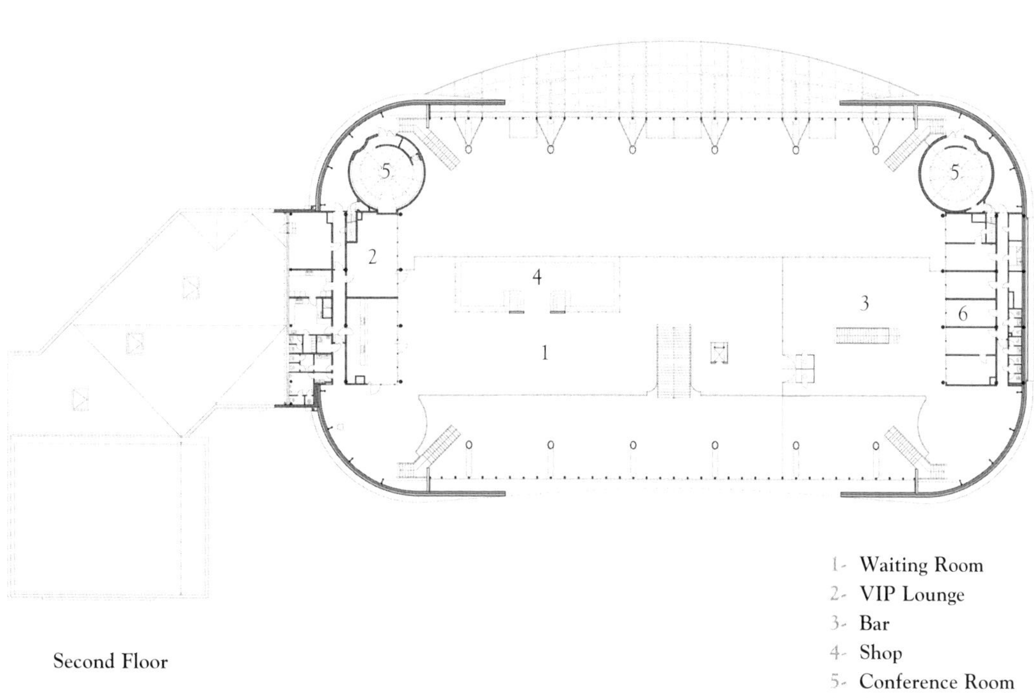

1- Waiting Room
2- VIP Lounge
3- Bar
4- Shop
5- Conference Room
6- Offices

Second Floor

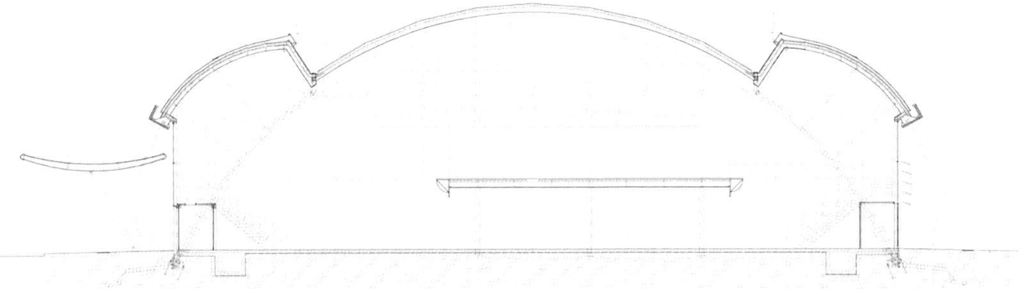

Cross Section

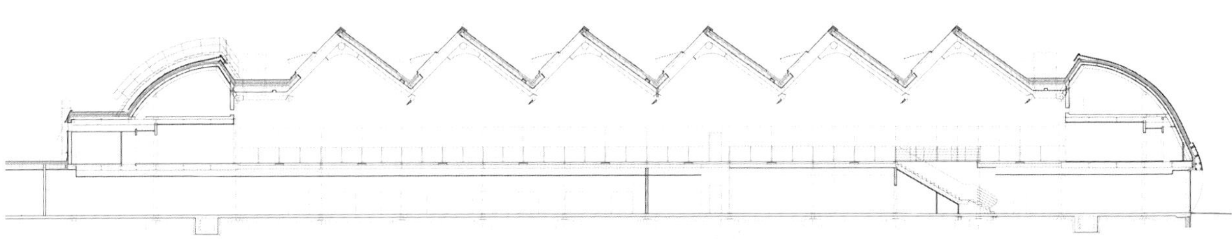

Longitudinal Section

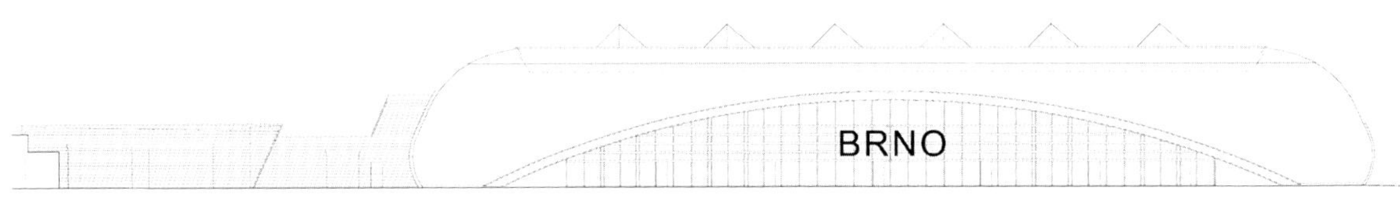

Front Elevation

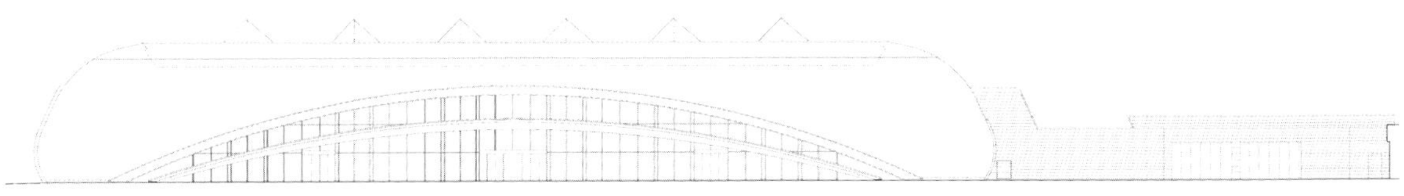

Rear Elevation

The new departures terminal is situated to the east of the central terminal in order to facilitate interconnection and combine the functions common to both terminals. The external space adjacent to the main corridor was expressly reserved for regular airlines, thereby adding to the functionality of the original building, situated to the north. The boarding area was set in the center, between Departures and Arrivals, for the greater convenience of the technicians and airline staff. The rectangular shape of the main entrance hall similarly enhanced the airport's operating conditions by opening up an expansive, flexible space.

Armor Shell

Very few buildings in the United Kingdom offer an array of flexible spaces suitable for various events on different scales. The Scottish Exhibition and Conference Centre in Glasgow sought to answer this need; it was the first covered structure in Europe with a seating capacity of 3,000. Despite budgetary restrictions, the architectural team came up with an economical solution that satisfies the above mentioned conditions in a complex uniting a commercial theater with an auditorium, exhibition halls, and conference venues. The design was inspired by the techniques of naval construction used on the legendary river Clyde, which runs through Glasgow. Its anatomical form serves as a protective shell and is divided by superimposed but continuous sections reminiscent of the armature of an armadillo (the popular nickname for the building). The sections in the form of an armor shell are covered with steel, reflecting sunshine by day and throwing light onto the river at night. The building's shape symbolically emphasizes its close surroundings, but it also evokes the city itself and has helped to consolidate Glasgow's worldwide reputation as a destination for businesspeople.

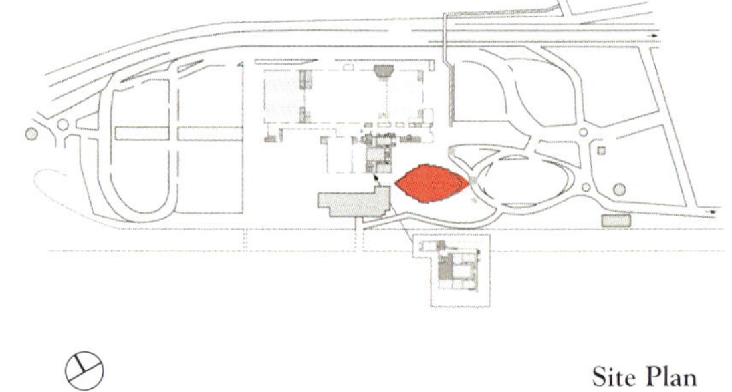

Site Plan

Client
Glasgow City Council

Type of Project
Convention center

Location
Glasgow, Scotland

Total Surface Area
215,816 square feet (20,050 m^2)

Completion Date
1997

Photos ©
Richard Davies

Glasgow, Scotland

SECC
Scottish Exhibition and Conference Centre

Foster + Partners

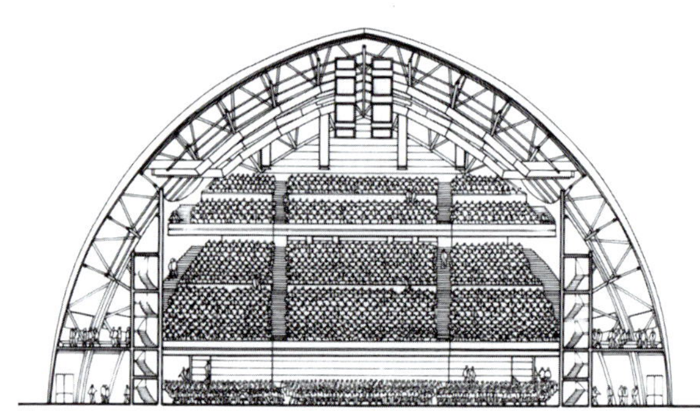

Cross Section

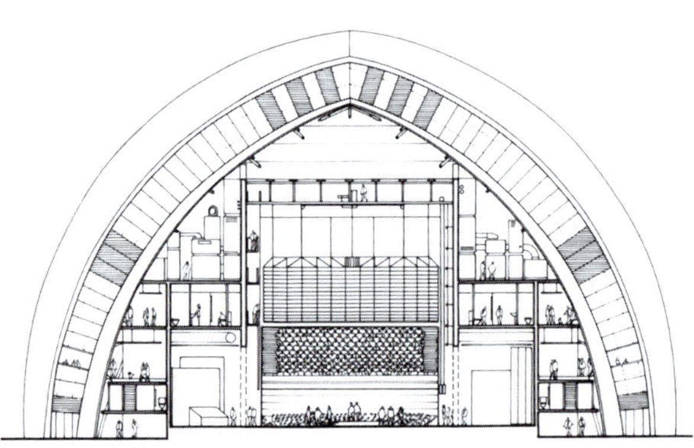

Cross Section

The commercial theater required a neutral but fully equipped and highly functional setting, capable of being transformed to host a wide range of events. The conference hall is very advanced in technical terms, boasting all the necessary backstage spaces and facilities, while trucks can pull up directly to the stage to unload. The main theater offers an electronic voting system for local elections, simultaneous translation services, projection systems, and sound control booths. Visitors enter the facility from the east of the structure, under a vault formed by the arch of the roof, and they can go straight into the conference hall (with a capacity of 300 people) or go upstairs to the first floor, which is linked to the main auditorium and a network of exhibition spaces.

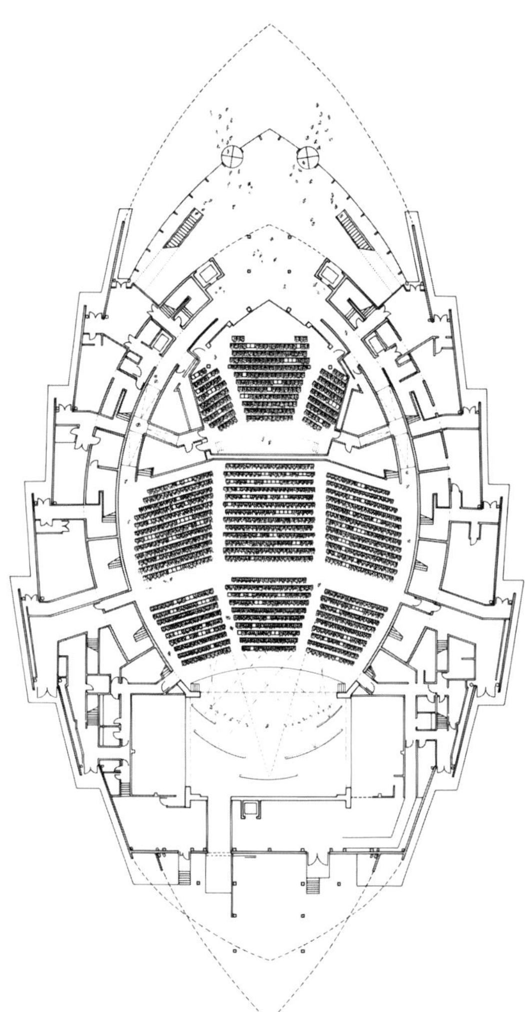

Ground Floor

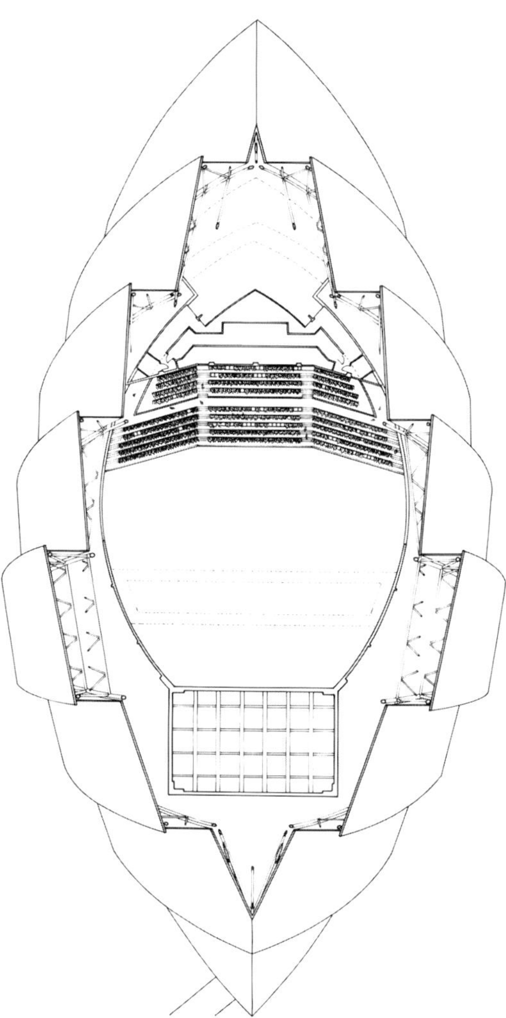

Second Floor

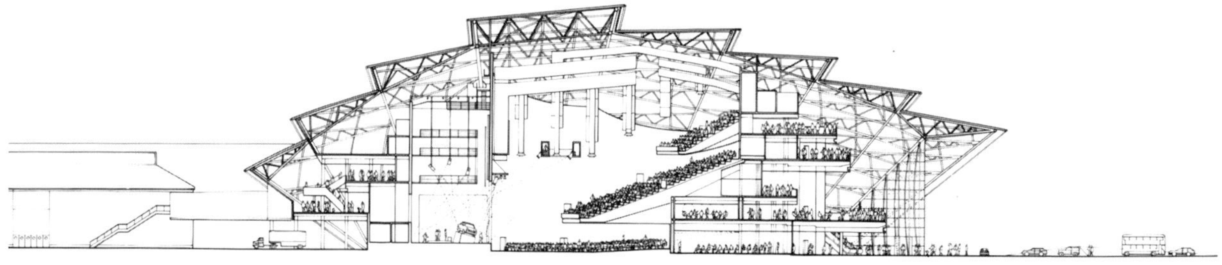

Longitudinal Section

The sobriety of the exterior is echoed in the interior through a concise interplay between the gray of the floors and walls, the purple of the seats, and the black of the ceiling.

Hermit Crab

An old windmill in the city of Caminha, in northern Portugal, was awaiting demolition to make way for a housing renovation scheme. During the project's design process, the possibility emerged of transforming the mill into a living and/or sleeping space, as a complement to one of the houses. There was little that could be added to the mill in architectural and spatial terms, so it was decided to spruce up the old structure, to adapt it to the new requirements of a domestic space. Inspired by the strategy of some birds, the architectural team went into the old windmill without touching the external walls and installed an internal roof made of aluminum. The intervention moved gradually from the interior of the structure, an area measuring a mere 86 square feet (8 m^2), to the exterior, where wood was the basic building material. In the entrance, the design of the staircase was predetermined by the presence of a rock, which reduced the habitable space still further. The remaining area was exploited in its entirety to make room for a bathroom and a sitting room, with a small couch that can be turned into a bed. According to the architects, the result is a wooden box fitted with the elements required to satisfy the basic needs of a home.

Client
Artur Domingues Santos

Type of Project
Housing

Location
Vilar de Mouros, Caminha, Portugal

Total Surface Area
215 square feet (20 m^2)

Completion Date
1995

Photos ©
Luis Ferreira Alves

Vilar de Mouros, Caminha, Portugal

Conversion of a Windmill

José Gigante

Preliminary Sketch

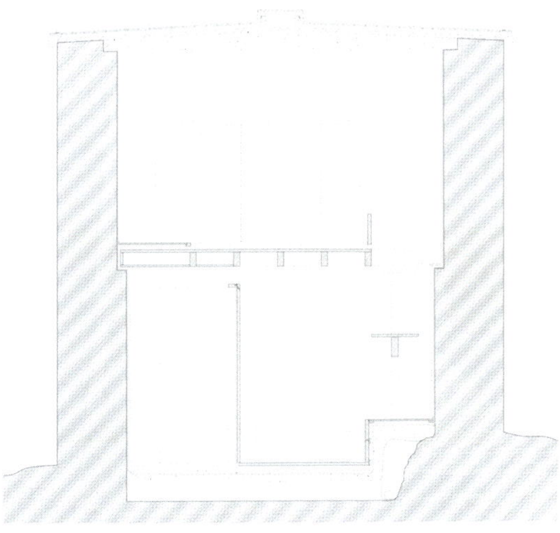

Cross Section

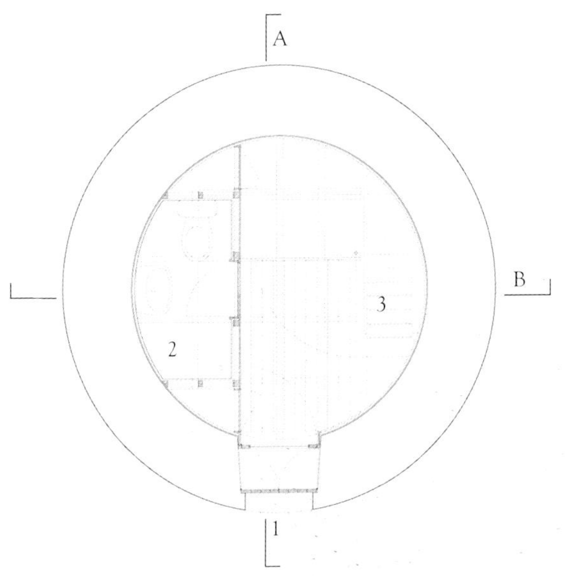

Ground Floor

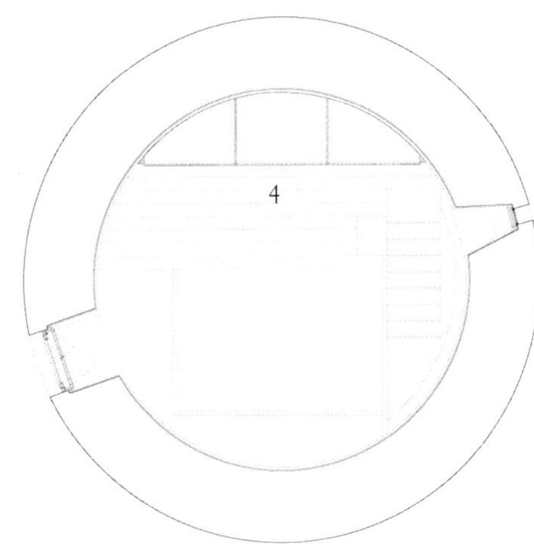

Second Floor

1- Entrance
2- Bathroom
3- Staircase
4- Sitting Room/Bedroom

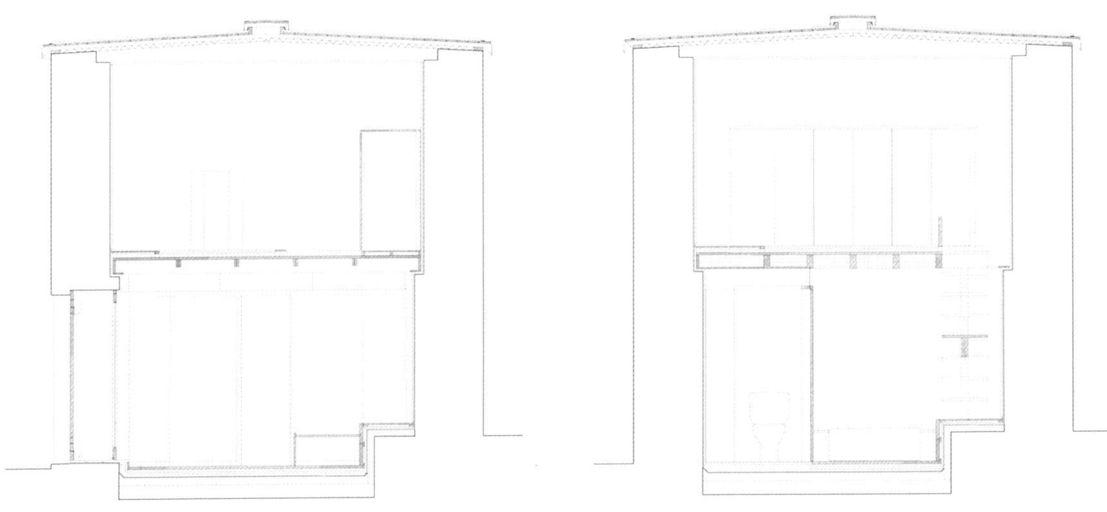

Section A

Section B

On the second floor, there is a closet and a couch bed that stretches out to one of the windows. The new design retained the original windows to benefit from the views of the surroundings, although they are separated from the wall to emphasize the idea of a refuge, as well as to highlight the contrast between old and new materials. It was important for the interior to effectively incorporate all the materials in a single unit. The exterior wall is so large—it occupies a greater surface area than the whole interior space, that it proved a fertile breeding ground for small parasitical plants.

Hermit Crab

An old pig stable in the Rhine Valley, dating from 1780, was the structure that gave rise to this project (hence the name!). The region's most characteristic features are its magnificent mountainous topography and the devastation wreaked by World War II, which left a landscape dotted with countless architectural ruins in its wake. The stable itself did not emerge unscathed from the bombardments and was refurbished on various occasions in the twentieth century. It was only in 2003, however, that the client decided to give the structure a radical twist and turn it into an exhibition room. A remodeling of the original building was financially unviable, due to the considerable deterioration of the structure, but it was also impossible to put up a completely new building, because it was situated close to a main road in the countryside. So, drawing inspiration from birds that take over nests that are not their own, the architects decided to build a new interior structure and leave the façades intact as a casing. The new interior area sets up an interesting contrast with the exterior, because both parts are covered with a roof that protects them from inclement weather. This resourceful intervention, which succeeds in harmoniously fusing a modern twenty-first-century vision with a rural eighteenth-century approach, earned its German architectural team several international prizes in 2005.

Site Plan

Client

Landgasthof Forelle GmbH&Co.KG

Type of Project

Exhibition room

Location

Eiswoog, Ramsen, Germany

Total Surface Area

226 square feet (21 m^2)

Completion Date

2004

Photos ©

Stefanie Naumann, Zooey Braun

Eiswoog, Ramsen, Germany

Saving the Bacon

fnp architekten

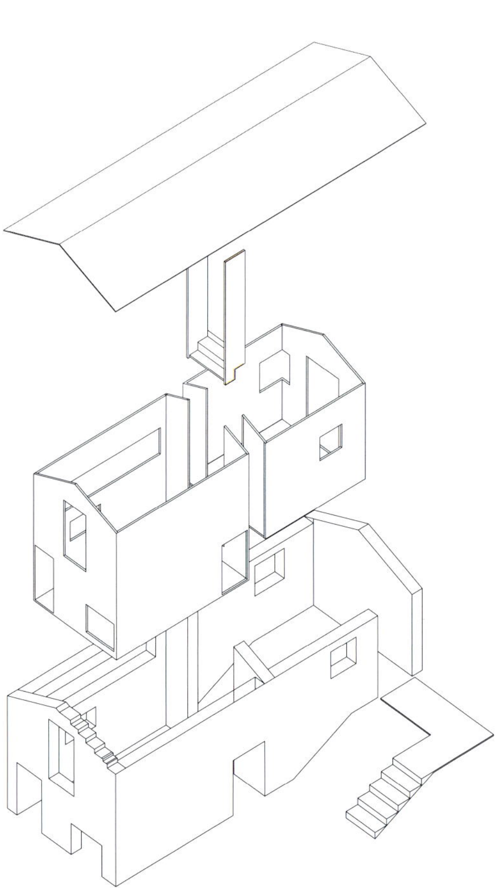

Exploded Axonometic

The new internal structure was built of wood and was installed from the top with a crane, leaving a slight space between the new core and the old stone wall. The apparently arbitrary position of the windows responds to the logic of the original granary i.e., a small exit for pigs in the lower right corner of the façade and a few windows that met the needs of their owners. However, these characteristics are used to the benefit of the new project and turn being in the exhibition room into a distinctive experience: visitors are quickly caught up in the light, color, and warmth of the atmosphere inside while also being fully aware that they have entered a centuries-old structure. Thus, the visitors experience the history of the building, which is no longer a ruin but has instead been transformed into a fascinating fusion of two very distinct ages.

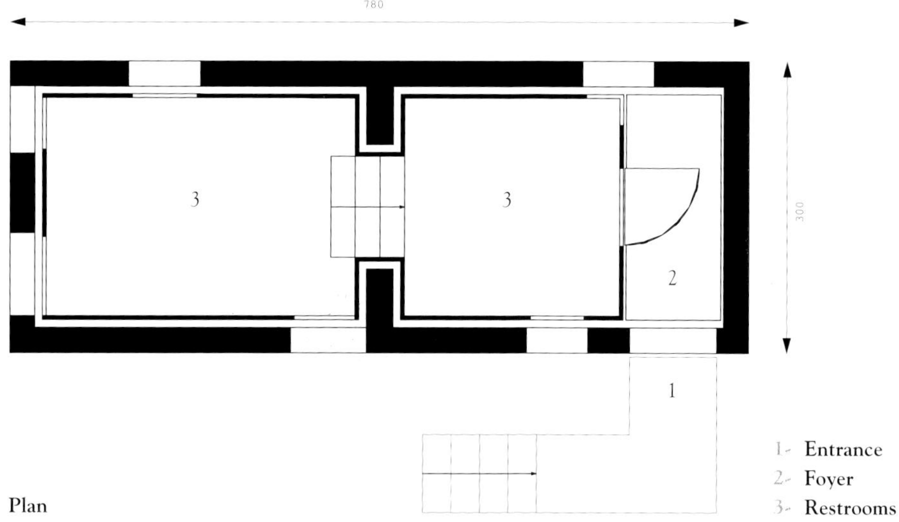

Plan

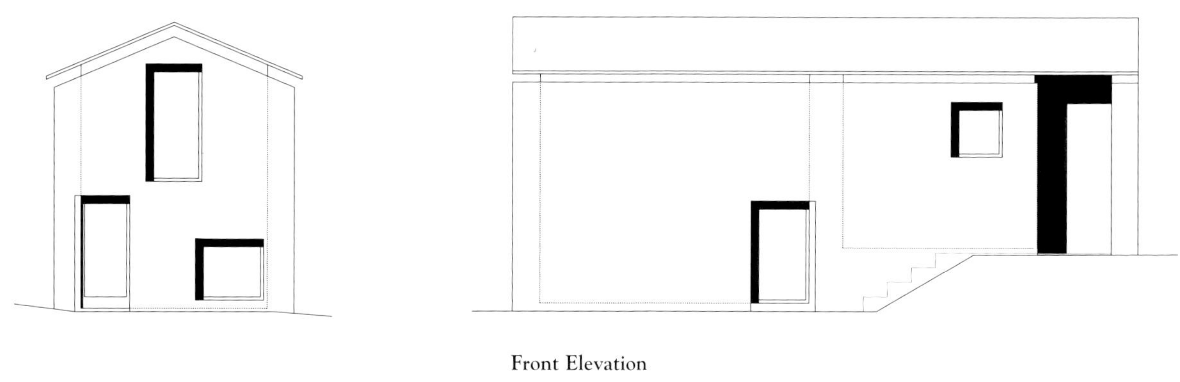
Front Elevation

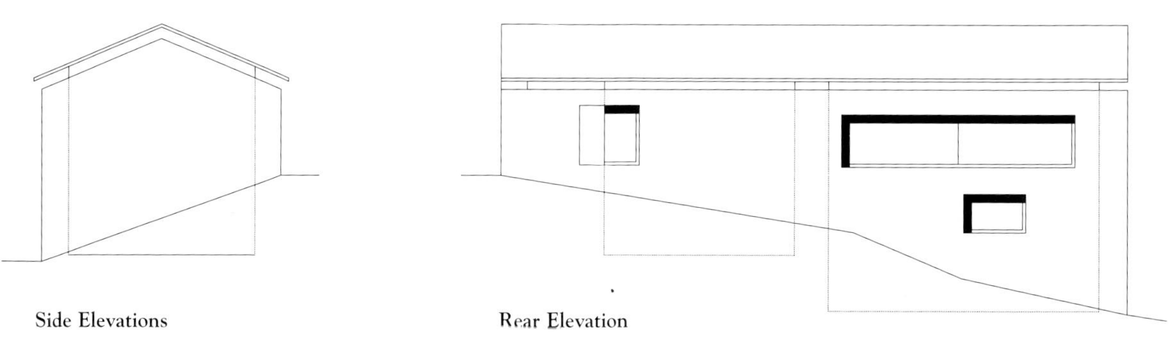
Side Elevations

Rear Elevation

Scales

The basis for this project was a preexisting shopping mall, set in the popular neighborhood of Apgujeong-dong in Seoul, South Korea. The building boasts an interior surface area of 236,653 square feet (21,986 m^2) and offers countless stores to the thousands of customers who visit it every day, attracted by its eclecticism and prestige. The building looked nondescript from the outside, however, and so scarcely lived up to the high reputation of the businesses established inside. So, in 2003, the Dutch architectural team UNStudio was commissioned to completely overhaul the building, and it focused on the need for a new, luxurious façade that would also be highly distinctive. The renovation of the façade's external tissue, inspired by snakes' changes of skin, was the thread running through the project. The most striking feature of this façade is the 4,330 discs that cover the entire structure like a second skin. Each disc or scale is made of glass and iridescent aluminum, a material that allows the colors of the façade to change constantly and alter the look of the building, according to the fall of natural or artificial light. This effect creates a fascinating, living surface that attracts attention and is in continuous transformation, according to the observer's viewpoint, the time of day, and the climatic changes. Furthermore, at night the façade can be adapted to special occasions, such as art installations and commercial events.

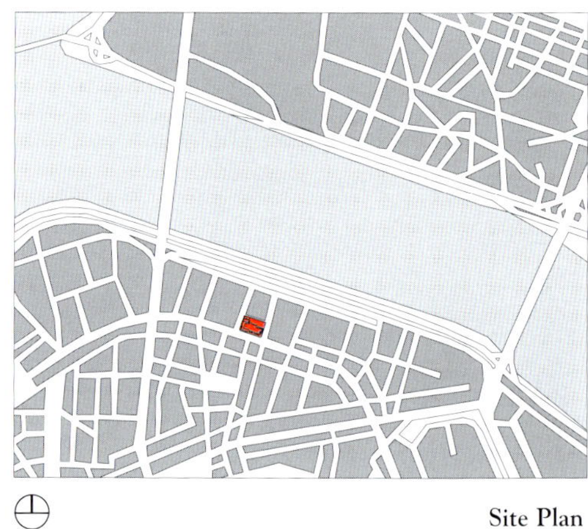

Site Plan

Client
Hanwha Stores Company

Type of Project
Shopping mall

Location
Seoul, South Korea

Total Surface Area
236,653 square feet (21,986 m^2)

Completion Date
2004

Photos ©
Christian Richters

Seoul, South Korea

Hall West Gallery

UNStudio

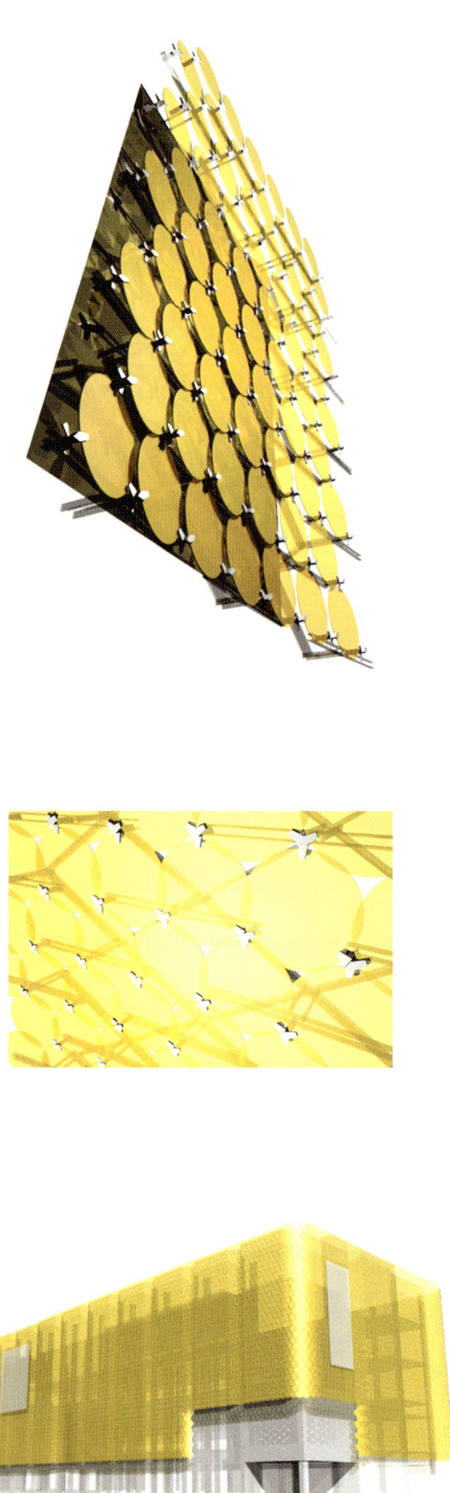

Studies for the Design of the Exterior Cladding

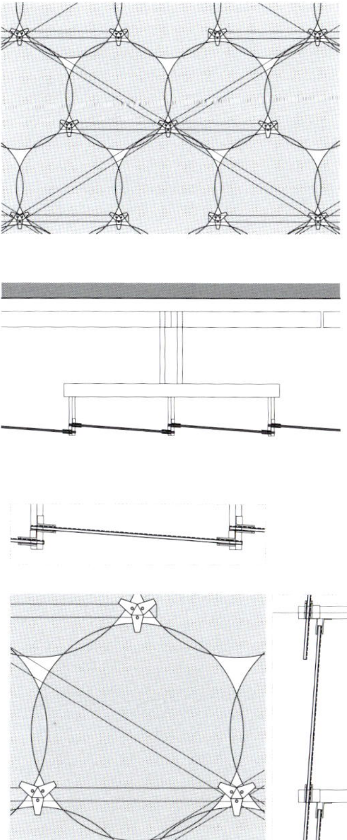

Details of the Supports for the Discs

The discs of aluminum and glass (laminated with a sandblaster) were attached to the concrete substructure that holds up the building by means of a metallic system that supports each piece. Before the building was finally constructed, various systems for coupling aluminum and glass had to be tested to achieve the desired impression both day and night. During the day, the outer skin changes color as the weather changes, as the scales are sensitive to variations in color and the projected reflections of light, which are beyond human control. At night, in contrast, the scales' sensitivity to light is manipulated by digital illumination, which plays with the material to create different effects. The façade does not function as a conventional screen, but it can interact with projected data, either through the reproduction of natural light filmed during the day or through the use of artificial light.

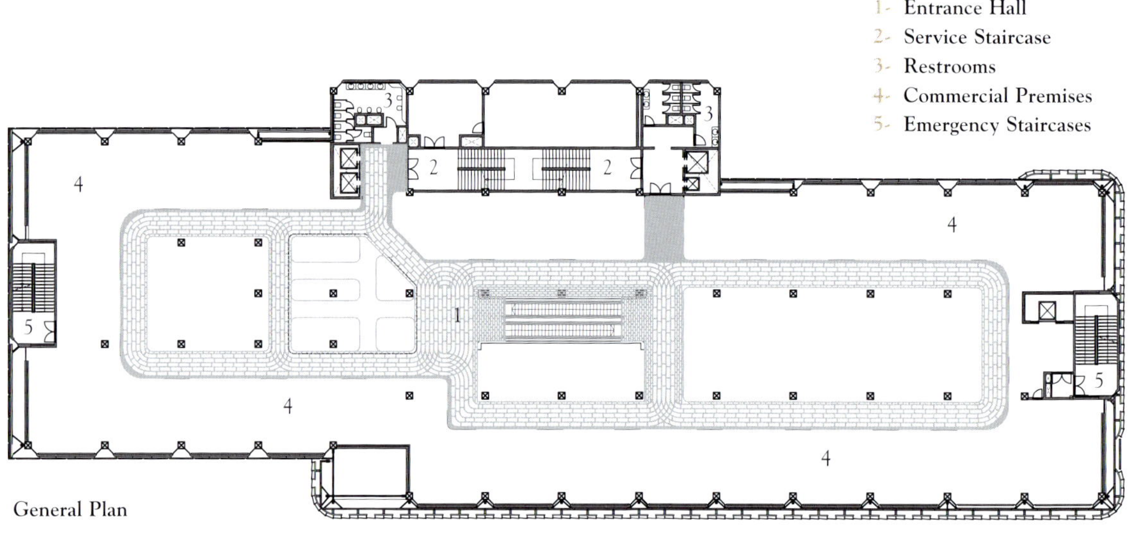

General Plan

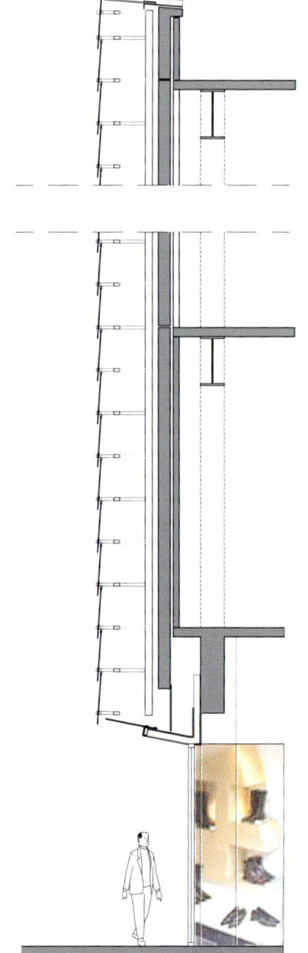

Section of the Outer Cladding of the Discs

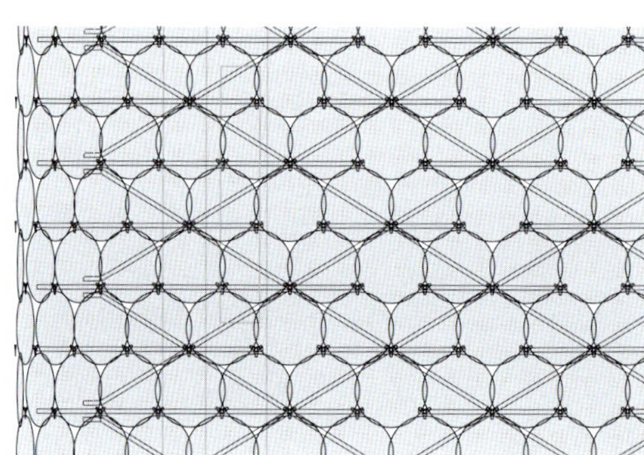

Partial Elevation of the Outer Cladding of the Discs

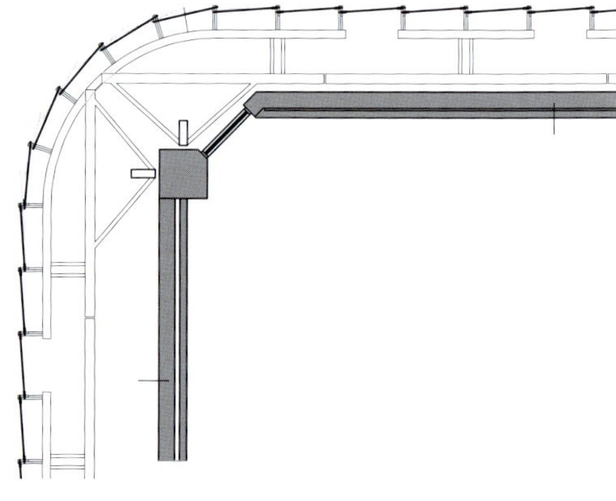

Plan of the Corner Cladding

Hair

The client chose this site in Laren, a quiet town in Holland, because it satisfied the basic criteria of being close to the market and not very far from the center. His idea was to demolish the preexisting house to construct a bigger, brand-new one with an innovative design adapted to the immediate surroundings. The architectural team wanted to explore an urban lifestyle in a rural setting, and this idea sparked the first plans, as well as the proposals for materials and the details. The result is a house characterized by the contrast between the style and the materials. On the one hand, the exterior walls made of reeds, inspired by the area's traditional houses, resemble the protective coat of an animal and evoke rural life, while, on the other hand, the copper roof and the curved windows allude to urban architecture. The house's main base is a wooden frame—set in the very foundations of the building—that is reminiscent of an upturned boat, with side windows that are also curved to establish closer contact with the exterior and to capture as much natural light as possible in the interior. The windows on the front are extended and divided upward almost from the base, with a height and rhythm similar to those of a waterfall—a feature also found on the wall separating the sitting room and the solarium from the interior of the house.

Site Plan

Client
Private

Type of Project
Family country house

Location
Laren, The Netherlands

Total Surface Area
2,153 square feet (200 m²)

Completion Date
2005

Photos ©
Casper Schuuring

Laren, The Netherlands

Laren House

MONK architecten

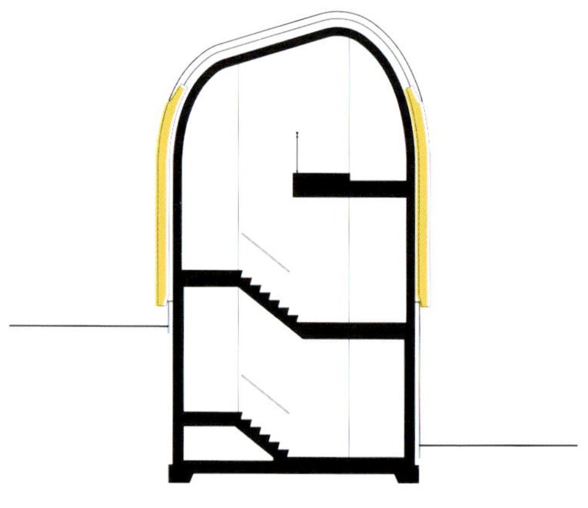

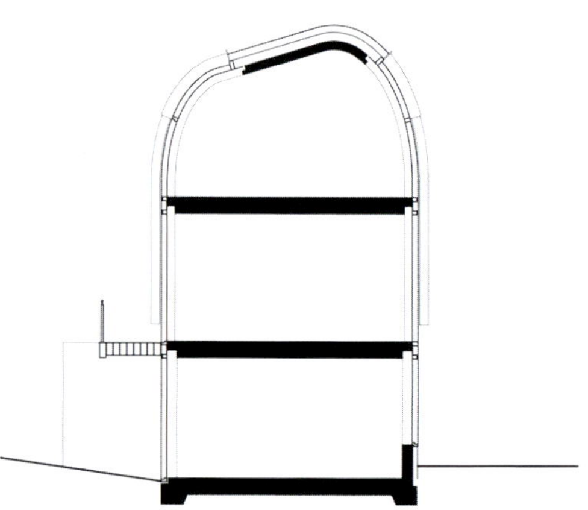

Cross Sections

The final plans were adjusted to the local building regulations for preservation, and so the original house's floor surface was used and only a few extra square yards were added to the new structure. The latter was therefore built exactly on the base of the old house, the only addition being the sun room to the rear (although an independent studio was also put up behind the main structure). The wood surrounding the windows is gray in color, and the glass used for the exterior of the solarium is separated from the reeds on the roof by superimposed wooden planks. To the rear of the house there is a pond, which is marked out with gray stones and has the same dimensions as the glass section of the solarium.

Longitudinal Section

Longitudinal Elevation

On the lateral façade three color elements define the different levels of the house and these set up a striking rhythmic effect in the ensemble.

Skin

This house is situated in the peaceful area of Burgenland in the city of Zurndorf, in eastern Austria, and at first sight it appears to be a structure set apart from all civilization. The client wanted a reasonably priced house that would adapt to its immediate surroundings (a fruit orchard on the outskirts of the city). The limited budget led to the use of unconventional resources in this case, a plywood roof and walls to achieve the desired form and dimensions. The analogy with elephant skin is derived from the application of a comprehensive insulating layer based on polyurethane, which establishes the heat levels appropriate to all types of weather, in the same way as does the skin of pachyderms. The house is divided into various levels, but at first sight it appears to be floating in a single mass above the ground, although it also reflects the typical homes of the region through the simple proportions of its façade and windows. In order to stay within budget and avoid the use of very costly materials, large expanses of glass were installed, uninterrupted by frames, and this had the added advantage of offering views of the orchard surrounding the house.

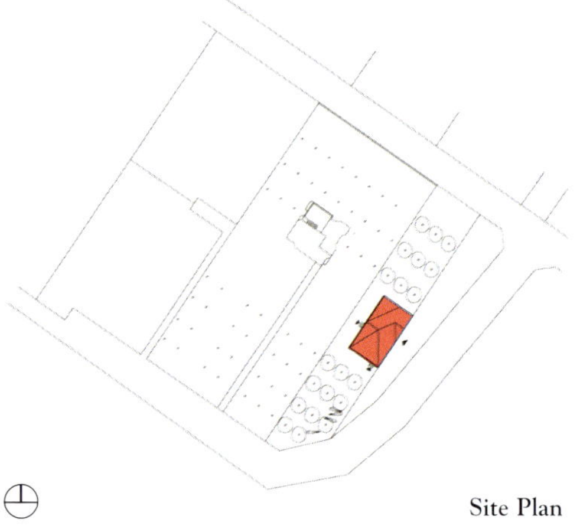

Site Plan

Client
Bettina Stimeder

Type of Project
Family home

Location
Zurndorf, Burgenland, Austria

Total Surface Area
1,076 square feet (100 m²)

Completion Date
2005

Photos ©
Margherita Spiluttini

Zurndorf, Burgenland, Austria

Elephant Skin House

PPAG Architects

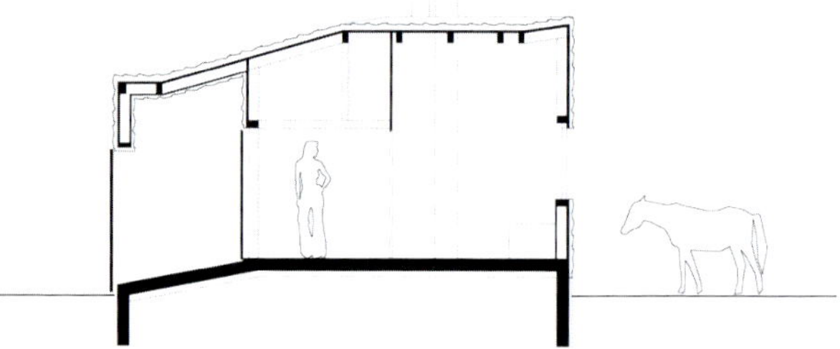

Cross Section

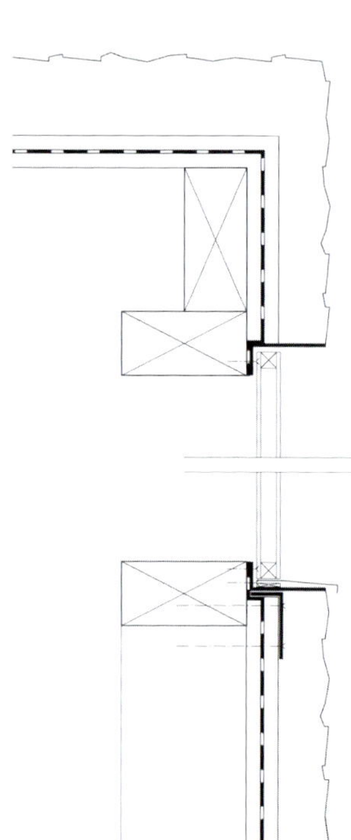

Detail of the Section of the Outer Cladding

Despite its thin walls 4 to 6 inches (10 to 15 cm) thick, this form of simple, economic construction complies with local regulations on thermal insulation.

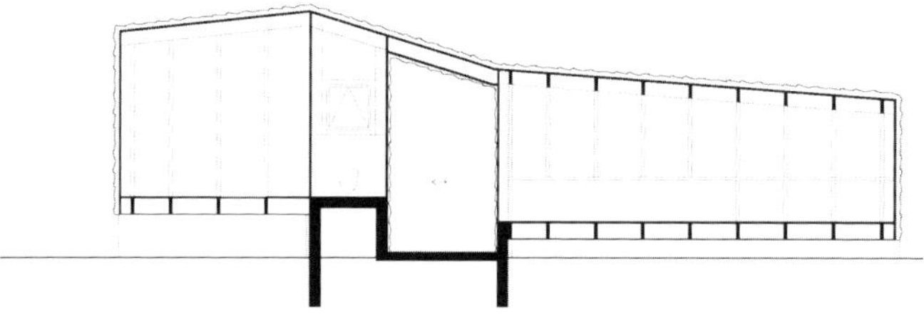

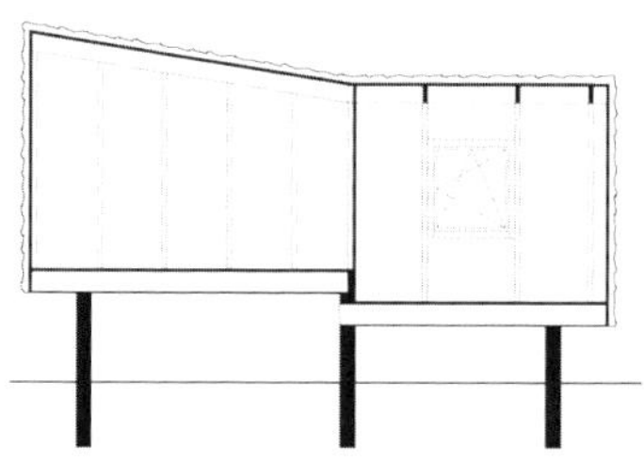

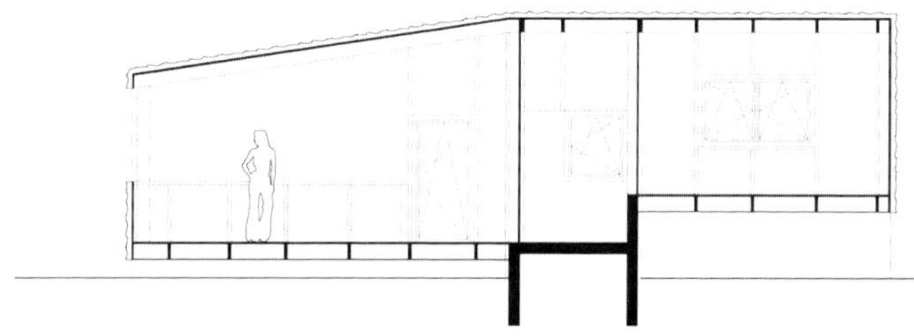

Longitudinal Sections

Cross Sections

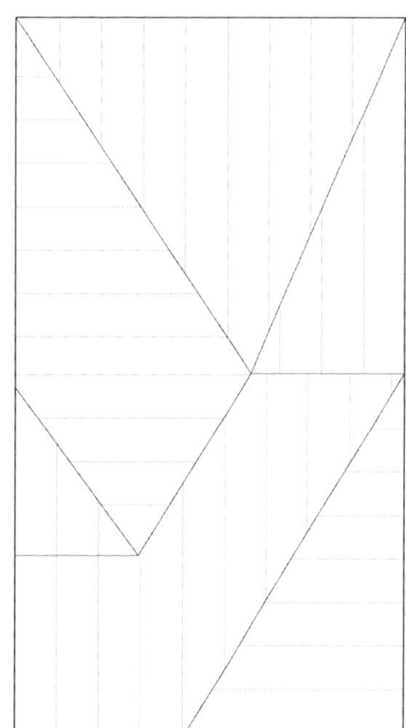

Plan of the Roofs

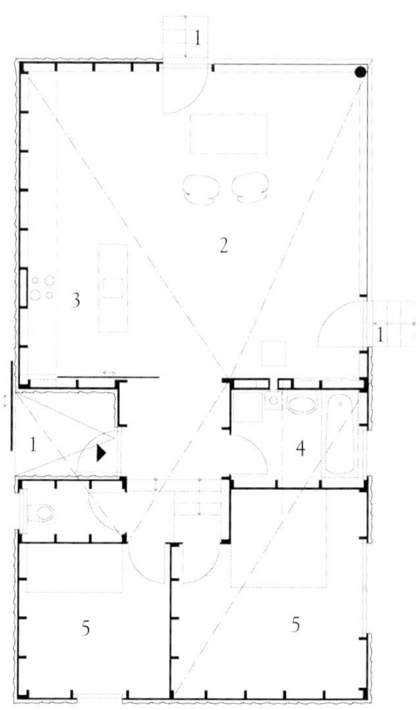

1- Entrances
2- Living Room
3- Kitchen
4- Bathroom
5- Bedrooms

Ground Floor

A central nucleus of service facilities, including the kitchen, was built on a solid substructure, along with a living area and, next to it, the bedrooms. The latter two areas are made of wood and are supported by longitudinal walls of slightly different heights. The cheap insulation method used for the house involved an outer skin consisting of a .08- to .12-inch (2 to 3-mm) layer of polystyrene foam on the walls and roof, which provides protection against UV rays. The dominant features of the interior are the plywood ends, the wooden doors and panels, and the roof beams. Shelves were integrated into the very structure of the bedrooms, between the wooden posts.

Skin

This temporary pavilion, built in 2005, represents a fusion of four different Norwegian museums: the National Gallery, the Museum of Decorative Arts and Design, the Museum of Norwegian Architecture and the Museum of Contemporary Art. The Kiss the Frog! pavilion was the first major joint project to explore the esthetic and transformation of several disciplines, such as architecture, art, and design. The architectural team wanted to merge these three areas into a single project and came up with an innovative concept using inflatable architecture, albeit on a scale never before undertaken with this method. The structure was inspired by the morphology and skin of a frog, including the color, and by the status this animal has acquired in the popular imagination through fairy stories. The project was based on the tale in which a prince under a spell turns into a frog, until a princess kisses him and restores his original form, and the two live happily ever after. The inflated pavilion connecting the old National Gallery with the new Museum of Art is 49 feet (15 m) high, with a total surface area of 21,582 square feet (2,005 m^2), providing a transition between the past and the present. Its organic form embodies the notion of transformation while also evoking the relationship between various artistic disciplines and questioning the boundaries between architecture, design, visual art, and popular culture.

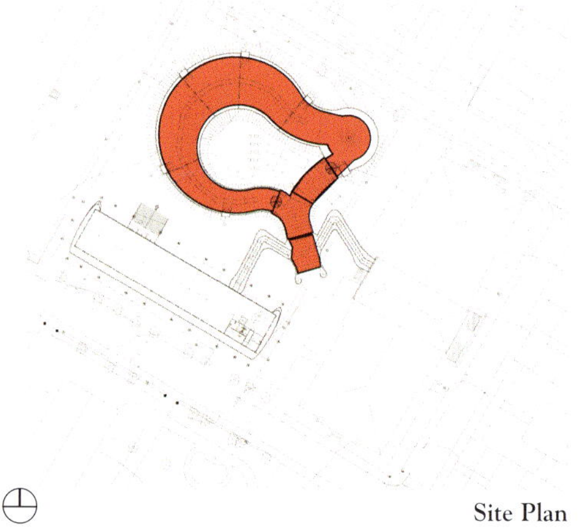

Site Plan

Client

National Museum of Art, Architecture, and Design

Type of Project

Temporary art pavilion

Location

Tullinløkka, Oslo, Norway

Total Surface Area

13,347 square feet (1,240 m^2)

Completion Date

2005

Photos ©

Eirik Førde, Martin Sunde Skulstad

Tullinløkka, Oslo, Norway

Kiss the Frog!
The Art of Transformation

mmw architects

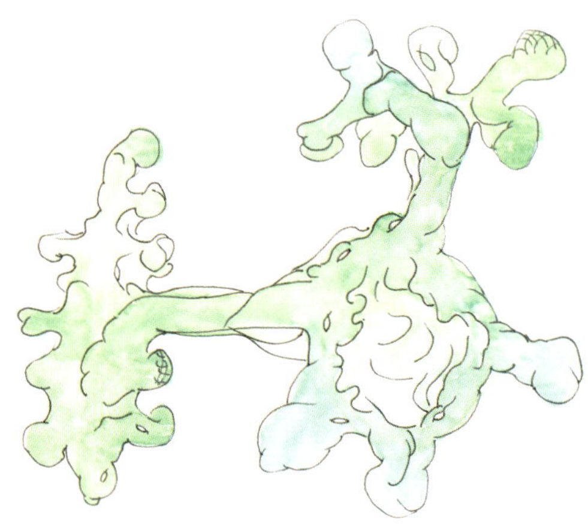

Preliminary Sketches

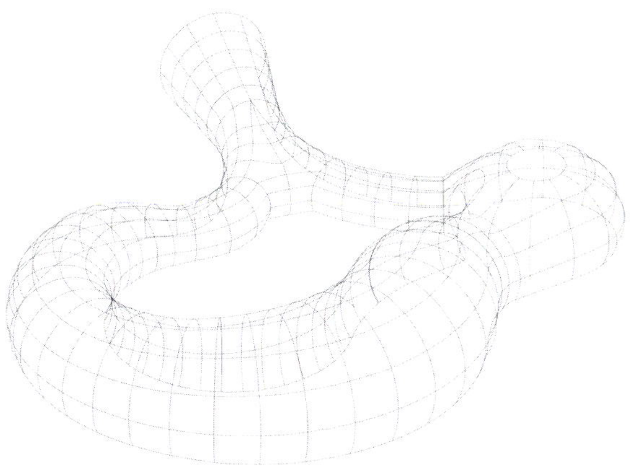

Structural Framework

The largest space in the pavilion has seven access points—a main entrance and six emergency exits—that are distributed along the length of a story with sinuous, organic forms. The structure is based on the principle of pneumatic tires—a self-supporting construction is inflated by increasing the pressure inside and is bounded by an external membrane. An enormous ventilator supplies constant fresh air to the interior and enables the structure to stay up. The green membrane is a PVC tissue with a protective, fireproof coating. The outer walls are concave planes that arise from the floor, and the interior is painted white, to allow different types of projections to be screened along the entire length of its structure, which offers an expanse of 656 feet (200 m) for temporary exhibitions.

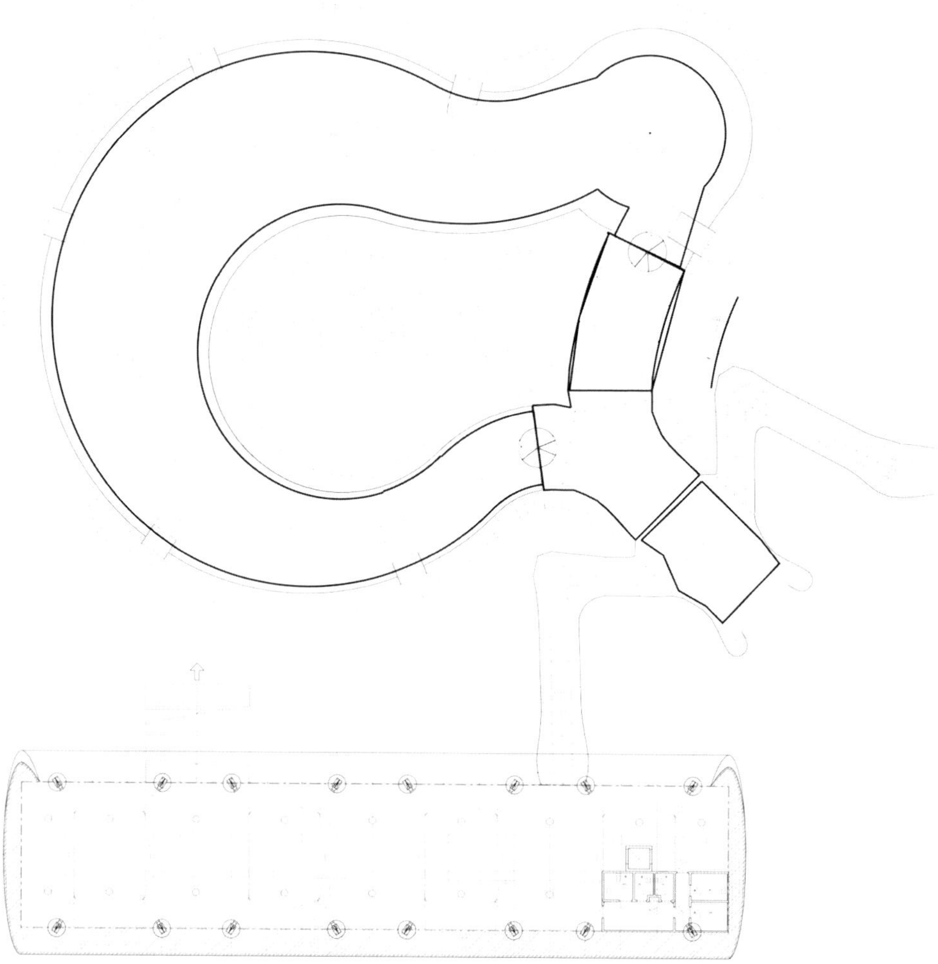

General Plan

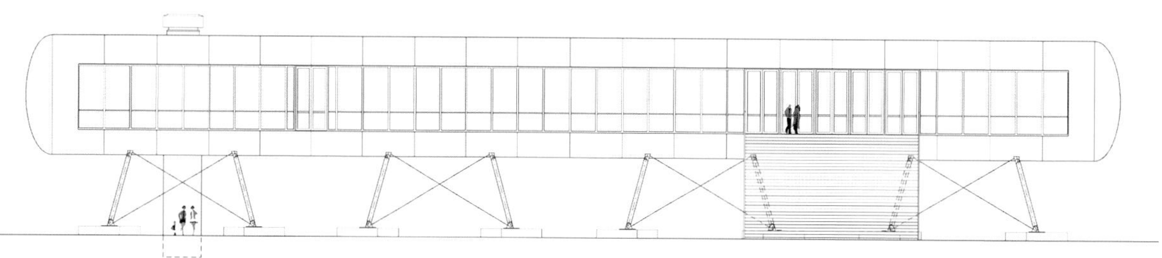

Front Elevation

The white finish and round surfaces of the interior conjure up a perfect setting for various types of exhibitions by creating a visual effect of infinity.

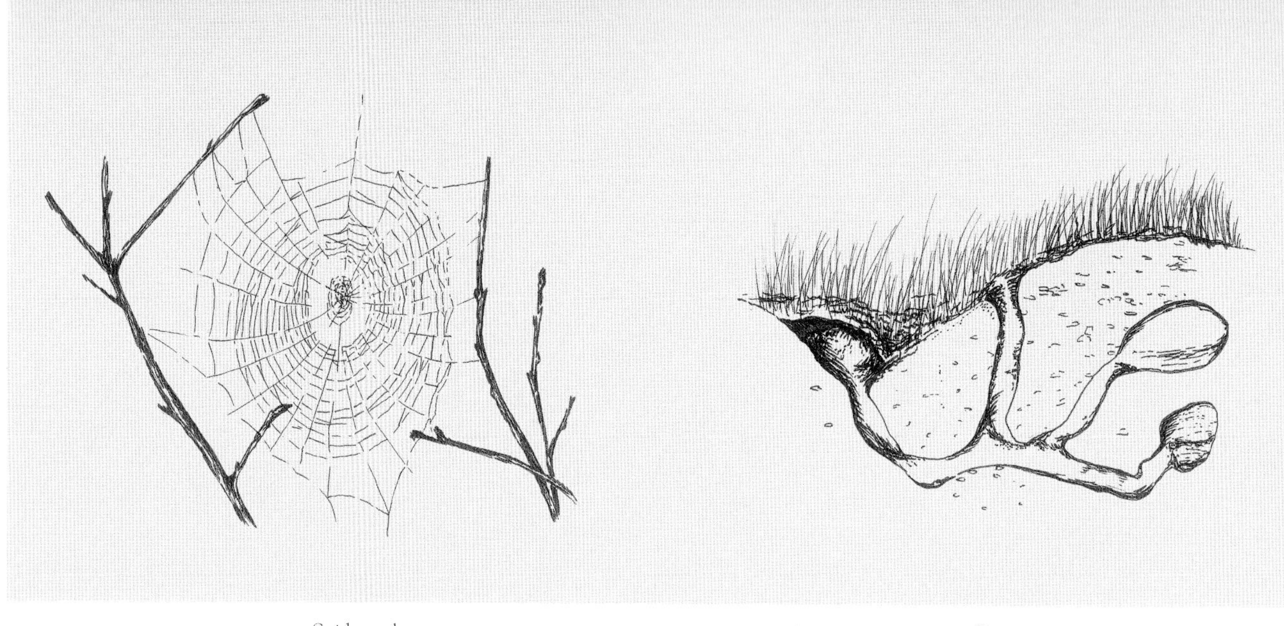

Spider web

Burrow

Animal Constructive Structures

Some animals display behavior and anatomical features specifically adapted to the building of structures, and more than a few secrete their own construction materials, such as wax and silk in the case of some insects, and saliva in birds. Many species pass their building skills from one generation to another, whether through genetic information, as with most animals, or through cultural transmission, as with human beings. It is precisely this capacity for transmission, complemented by mankind's enormous constructive imagination and great capacity for innovation, that has allowed human shelters to evolve to such extremes of complexity and richness. In these terms, the animal constructions presented below stand out on account of the economy of means, sustainability, and originality characteristic of this naïve but pure architecture, the product of an apprenticeship based on a technique of trial and error applied throughout the life of each individual. Although it is true that many of these structures are distinguished by their simplicity and rusticity, others can surprise us by their complexity or beauty.

Spider webs display an astonishing versatility, apart from their resistance (the thread can be five times stronger than a steel filament of the same thickness) and their flexibility (the silk produced by a spider can be stretched by up to one-third of its original length without breaking). Spiders weave their webs to trap their prey, to create entrance doors to dens in the ground, to move about with the help of the wind, to make cocoons for its eggs, and even to court a potential partner. One curious variant is the web of the water spider, which is woven under the water in the form of a bell, amid aquatic plants, before being filled up with air bubbles. To achieve this, the spider makes several journeys to the surface to trap bubbles between its legs, with the aid of hydrofugal hairs. As the reserves of air are used up, the spider restocks it with regular trips to the surface.

Less elegant, but equally mysterious, are the animal constructions burrowed out of rock, wood, or soil. Moles are the standard-bearers of gallery builders. Their burrows reveal their presence aboveground through a mound of earth, while their complex internal structure is distinguished by a warren of tunnels arrayed around an entrance. The concentric galleries, spread over different levels, intercommunicate by

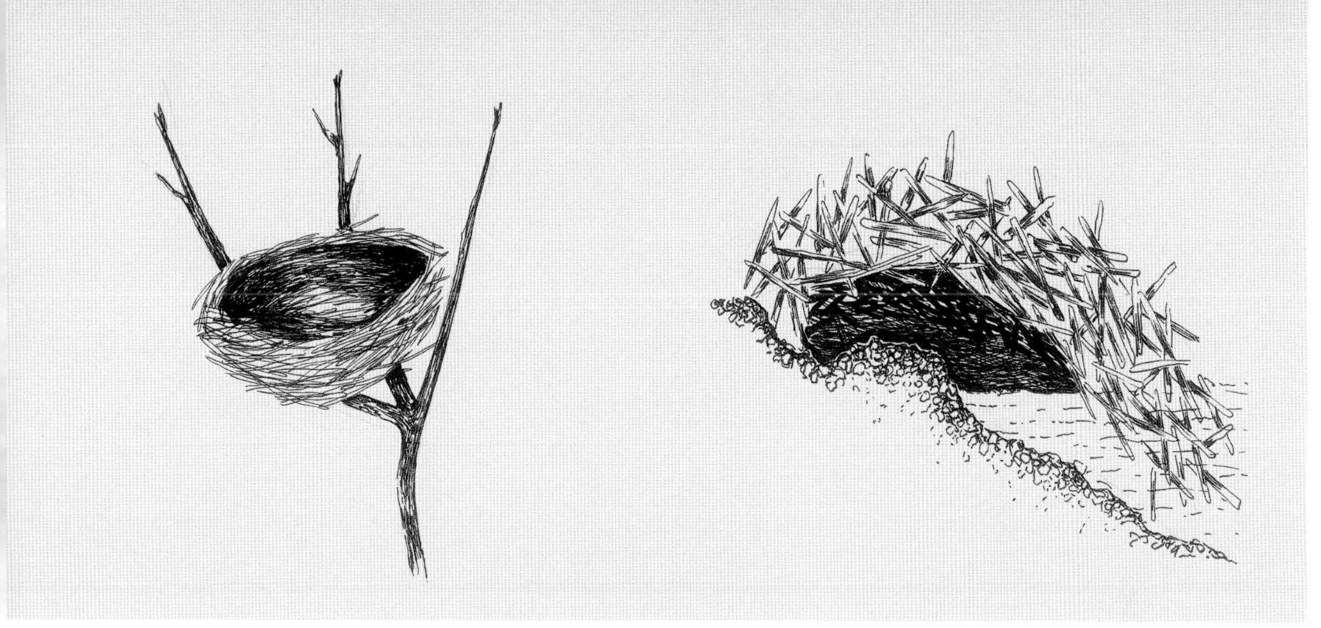

Nest

Beaver Lodge

means of a network of channels of varying length (some of them cul-de-sacs). The galleries, with a total length of around 49 feet (15 m), are marked by rest chambers, bypasses, emergency exits, etc. The breeding chamber lies at the crossroads of various tunnels, to facilitate flight in case of danger. For some animals that live underground, the renewal of air is of paramount importance. This is the case with the prairie dog, a rodent that builds two entrances to ventilate its burrow. The entrance tubes are inclined in the form of a funnel, surrounded by a mound of earth to protect it from floods caused by heavy rain or to provide a lookout point.

Nests come in countless shapes and sizes. The hanging nest of the penduline tit is like an egg or bag built with twigs, animal or vegetable fibers, spider webs, fluffy seeds, and other materials. One significant detail: this nest has two entrance tunnels, the biggest of which is false and serves solely to deceive potential predators, while the much smaller real entrance is unobtrusive.

When swallows build their nests, they use their sticky saliva, which hardens when dried and so becomes an effective glue. The salivary glands of swifts are so active that their secretion alone is sufficient to build their nests (highly prized in the Far East for making bird's nest soup).

Some types of tree frogs (*Hyla sp.*) build round nests on the edge of a stream to lay their eggs. To do this, the male spins around on a specific spot to rub away the mud and create a depression, before making it deeper by extracting more mud with his snout. He then tramples down the opening to form a wall up to 2.7 inches (7 cm) high.

Finally, we cannot overlook beavers, who skillfully build houses with doors that form ingenious security systems and open under water. These doors give onto a rising gallery that leads to a spacious chamber with a flat floor, shrouded in moss and dry grass, and a perforation that communicates with the exterior, allowing the beavers to breathe by letting air penetrate inside. To shield the entrance galleries from view, beavers often build veritable dikes with tree trunks and branches, thereby forming a pool that totally hides the main entrance to their home.

Nest

Silbersee is a nature reserve situated on the northern outskirts of Hochheim, between Wiesbaden and Frankfurt, and it is home to large numbers of birds and animals. The bird observatory—better known as "the nest" on account of its shape—formed part of a far-reaching project undertaken inside the natural park. The main aim of the intervention was to allow visitors and birdwatchers to enjoy the natural setting without disrupting it. As it is forbidden to enter the park's ecosystem, it was decided to build an observatory—in this case, a bird's nest for visitors—that would make it possible to examine the ecosystem without coming into direct contact with it. The nest is now considered an integral part of the park's landscape and ecosystem, as well as a harmonious construction within the nature reserve, which is a reproduction of a Rhineland setting—and so the observatory is in fact no more artificial than the rest of the nature reserve. The observatory resembles a large bird's nest resting on the branches of a tree, and it offers views of the lake, set behind the main pier, as well as providing a link with a platform from which visitors can enter into the world of birds from the lake itself.

Site Plan

Client

RheinMain GmbH Regional Park

Type of Project

Observatory in a nature reserve

Location

Hochheim, Germany

Total Surface Area

215 square feet (20 m^2)

Completion Date

2001

Photos ©

Eicken & Mack Fotoproduktion
www.eickenundmack.de

Hochheim, Germany

Vogelnest Observatory

Freie Architekten

Preliminary Sketch

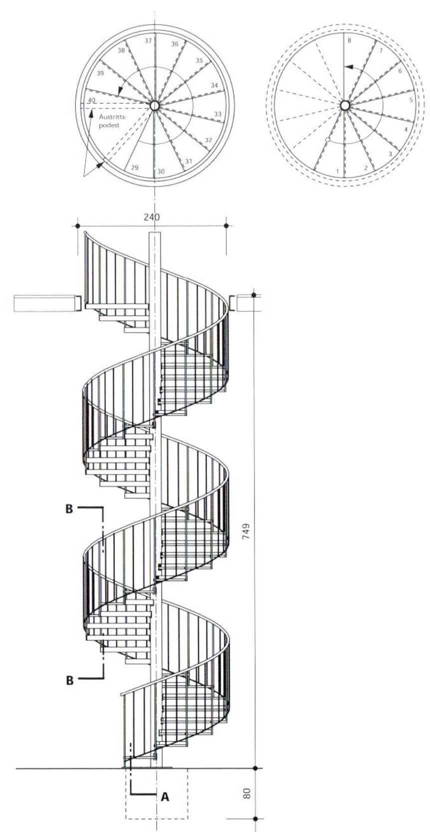

Construction Details of the Staircase

The observation platform stands 25 feet (7.5 m) above the ground, held up by eight supports made of laminated, veneered wood, ranging in diameter from 22 to 28 feet (6.8 to 8.5 m) and set at various angles and heights around the platform. The supports rest on two parallel strips with four steel points in the form of a fork that evoke the branches of a tree and hold the wooden observatory on the top of the structure. The platform, 20 feet (6 m) in diameter, is crowned by a steel staircase that links the base to the upper part of the observatory. The height of the nest-observatory enables visitors to enjoy panoramic views of the entire park, and they can also catch glimpses of the landscape through the ring supports as they go up the staircase.

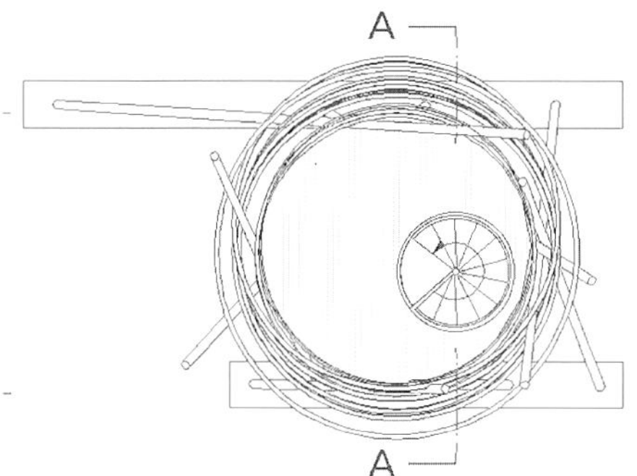

Plan

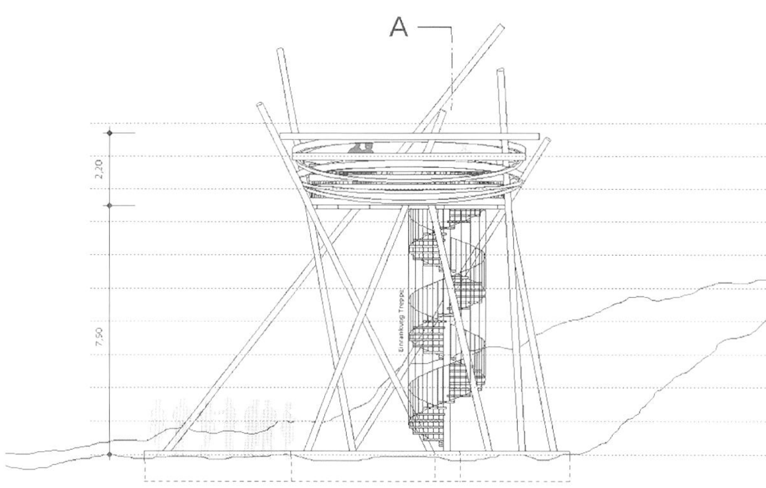

Cross Section

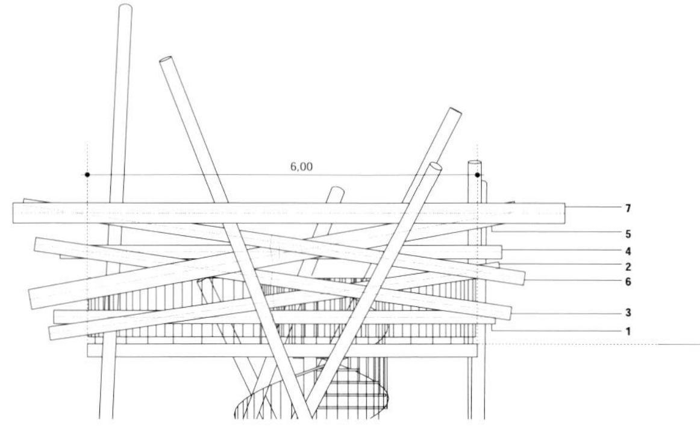

Detail

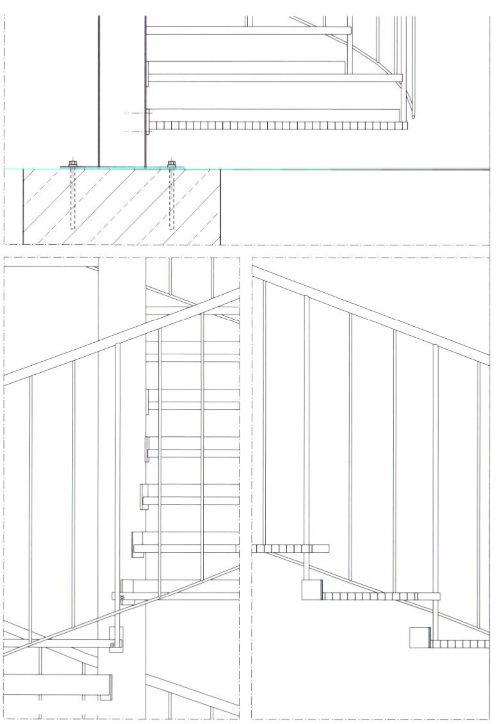

Construction Details of the Staircase

Once the staircase was put in place, the ring supports were placed at different heights and angles, to give the structure an irregular and therefore more dynamic rhythm.

Nest

The design of this house-tower was inspired by the architect's childhood memories of Arkansas and pays homage to a tree house built by his grandfather. This site is characterized by its arid soil, which made it difficult to find a tree on the 60-acre (23-ha) lot able to support a structure. The solution was the construction of a house that rises up like a bird's nest between oak and walnut trees, joining up the spaces between the trees in the wood to create the effect of interlocking pieces. This concept is evident in the lower part of the design, where a framework of white oak filters and reflects the light while also serving as a support for the house on top of it. When seen from the front, the framework looks like a translucent base bearing the weight of the upper part of the structure. When one walks around the building, however, the spaces in the framework seem to connect the tower with the ground, while establishing a contrast with the steelclad panels that form the eastern part of the structure and rise above the trees. These panels evoke the white metallic cladding of agricultural buildings and fit in naturally with the pattern of the woodland around it.

Site Plan

Client
James Keenan

Type of Project
House in a tower

Location
Fayetteville, Arkansas

Height
269 square feet (25 m^2)

Completion Date
2000

Photos ©
Tim Hursley

Fayetteville, Arkansas

Keenan Tower

Marlon Blackwell

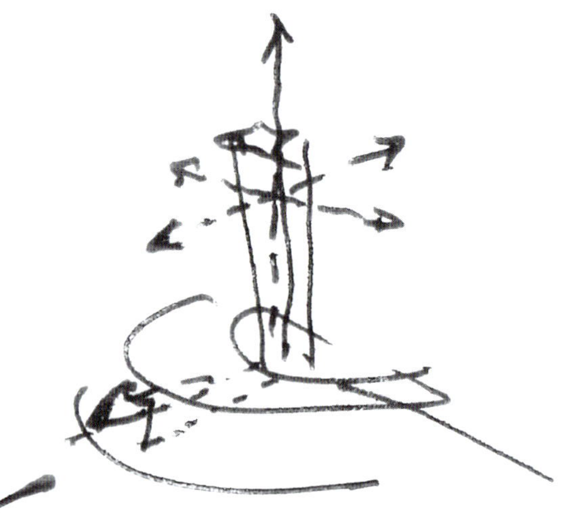

Preliminary Sketches

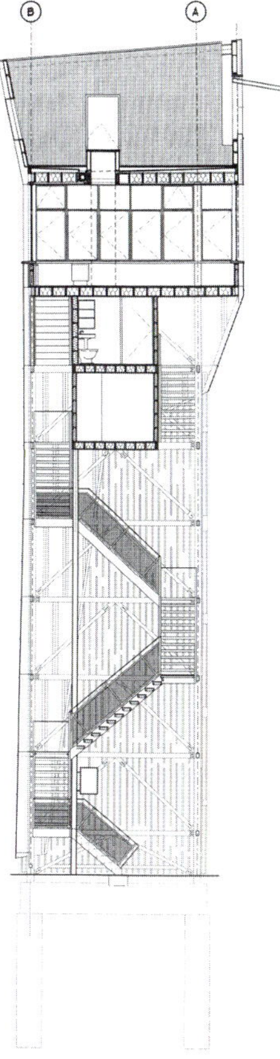

Cross Section

The land on which this structure was built is covered with pebbles, and there is a change in sound on reaching the well of the staircase leading up to the house, because here the ground is strewn with crushed pecan shells. The house is simple in functional terms: it has an interior space with an expansive view of the horizon in all directions and an outdoor area with a projecting roof that frames the earth and sky in a single image. So, there is an immediate sense of contact with the natural environment, and the house is also ideally located to appreciate changes in the solar and lunar cycles and in the seasons, as the structure faces all four cardinal points.

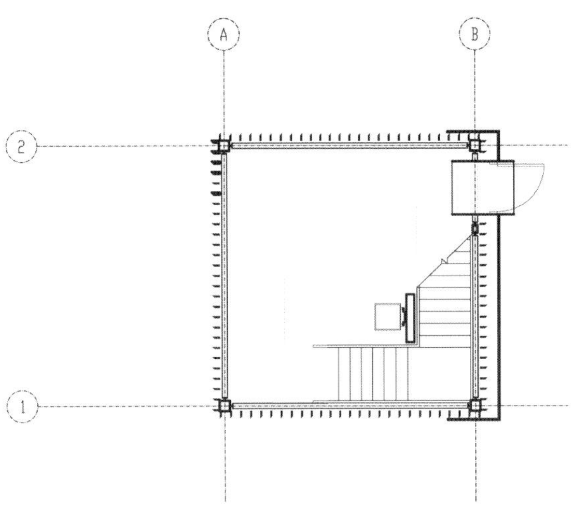

Ground Floor, Entrance

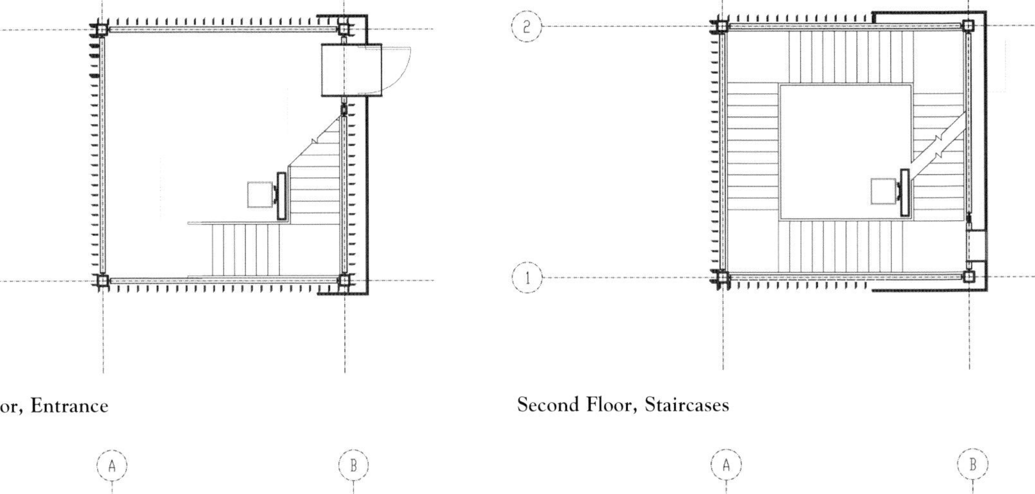

Second Floor, Staircases

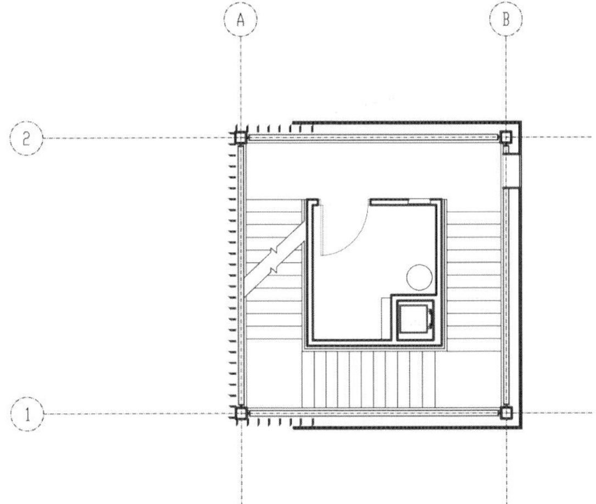

Third Floor, Machines

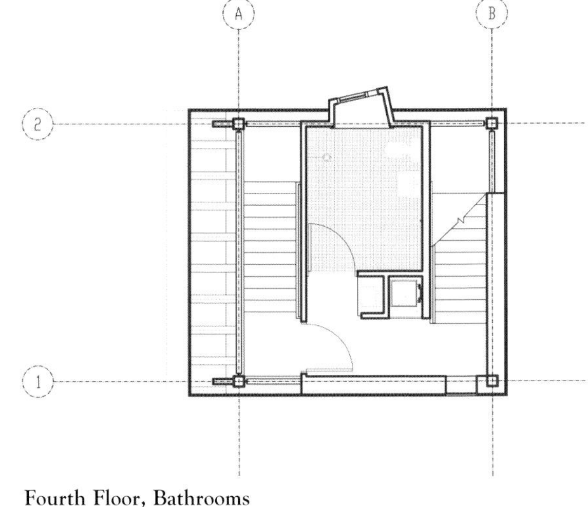

Fourth Floor, Bathrooms

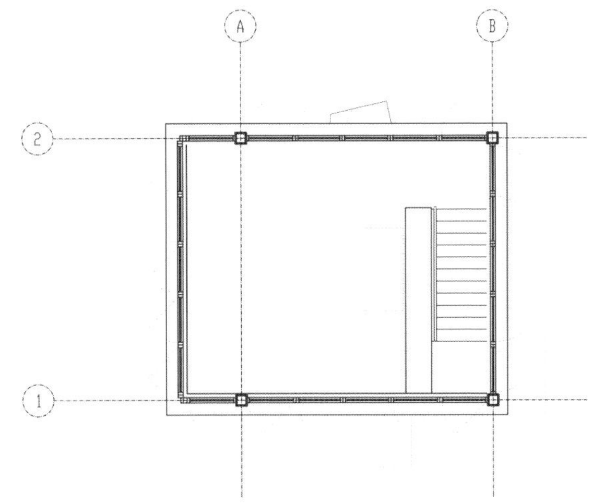

Fifth Floor, Observatory

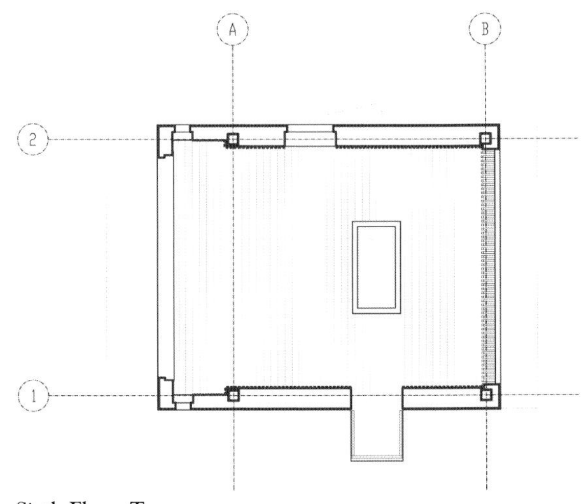

Sixth Floor, Terrace

Spider web

The floating Mur Island is a sophisticated structure specially designed for the events accruing from Graz, Austria's being named one of UNESCO's Cultural Capitals of Europe for 2003. The project was initially conceived as a temporary structure in which various events and cultural encounters would be organized to exploit its capacity as a multifunctional public space. However, the structure has grown into a permanent and emblematic landmark, because of its growing popularity and distinctive design that provides a solid link between two sides of the city, like a spider web spread out over the river. The main aim was to create an island that would link the city with the river and thus provide a new space for interaction, adventure, and artistic creation. The island's modular design, evoking an egg in a net, allows it to be converted into a theater or a public space or square with a capacity of 300 people. From inside, the river and the city appear in a new light, and the netlike structure brings the two together. All the activity spaces in the interior are linked by a spiral tunnel that echoes the island's central form, while two access ramps connect the island to the banks. The intervention also serves as a bridge spanning the 154-foot (47-m) width of the Mur River, and as a lighthouse, thanks to the blue light that shines at night.

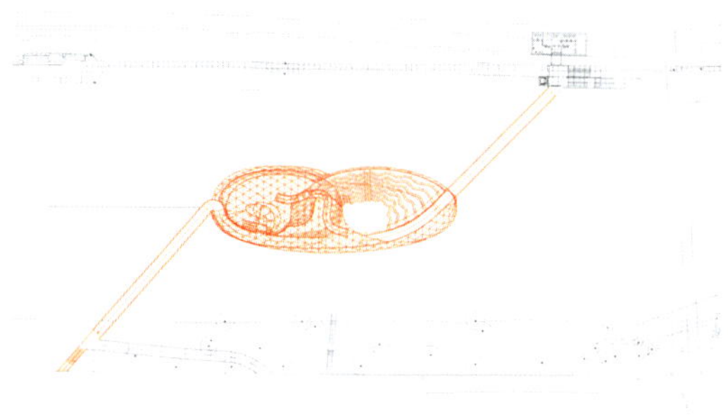

Site Plan

Client

Graz 2003

Type of Project

Multifunctional space

Location

Graz, Austria

Total Surface Area

10,301 square feet (957 m^2)

Completion Date

2003

Photos ©

Acconci Studio, Elvira Klamminger, Harry Schiffer

Graz, Austria

Mur Island

Acconci Studio

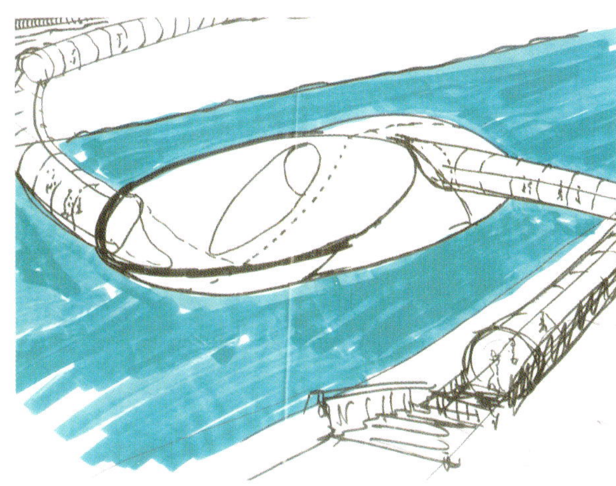

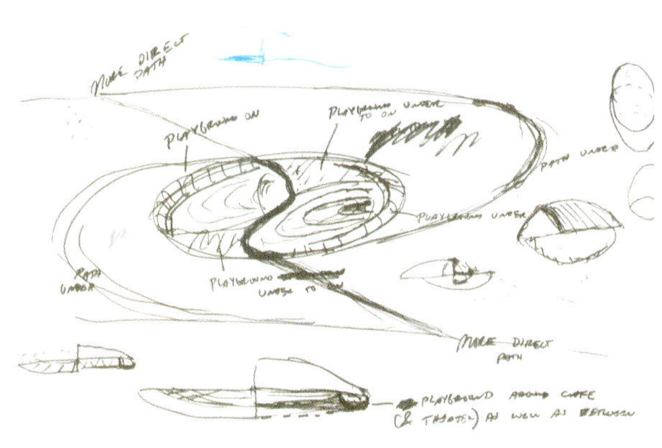

Preliminary Sketches

The island rests on a platform built of steel and glass, while the base rests on two quays, fixed to the banks by cables that cannot be seen from inside. The use of transparent materials intended to convey an absence of borders between the building and the water, and thus create the sensation of floating gently inside an air bubble. The spiral form is divided into two areas, one covered and one uncovered, like the two valves of an open shell. The uncovered section can serve as a square or theater, with various possible configurations of bleachers that give visitors a more passive or active role as required. The section covered with glass contains a café, which can be reached from below or from above, while the children's playground is endowed with a maze and a slide (which links the theater with the café).

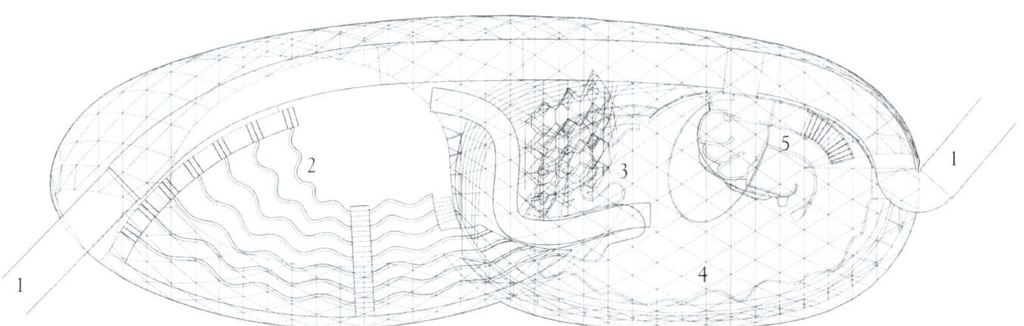

General Plan

1- Entrance
2- Outdoor Theater
3- Playground
4- Café
5- Restrooms

Longitudinal Section

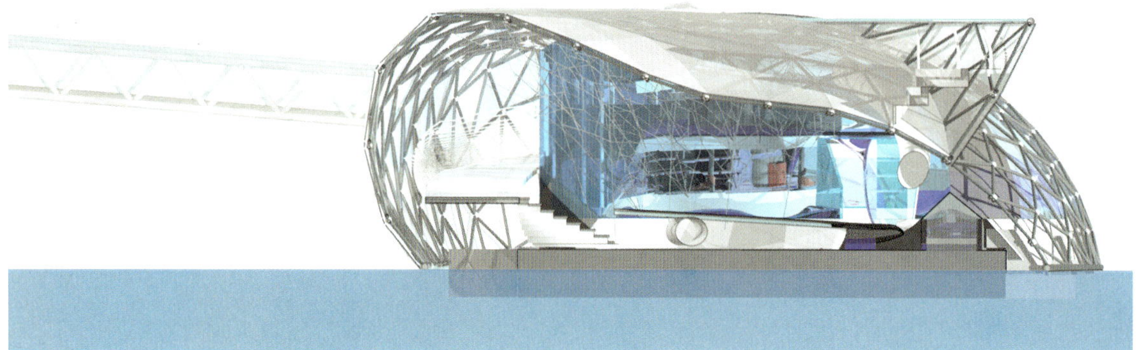

Cross Section

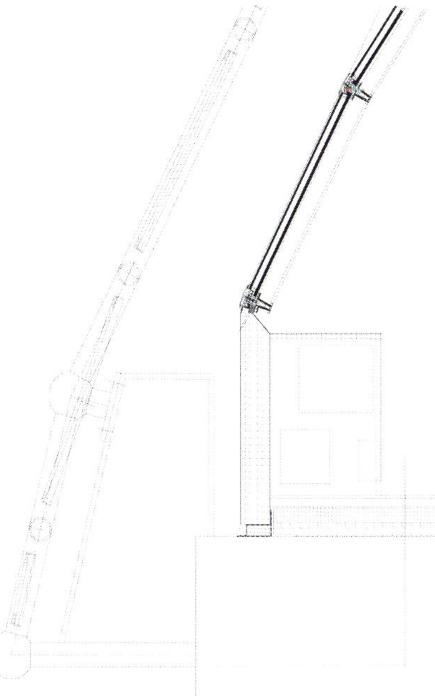

Detail of the Cladding

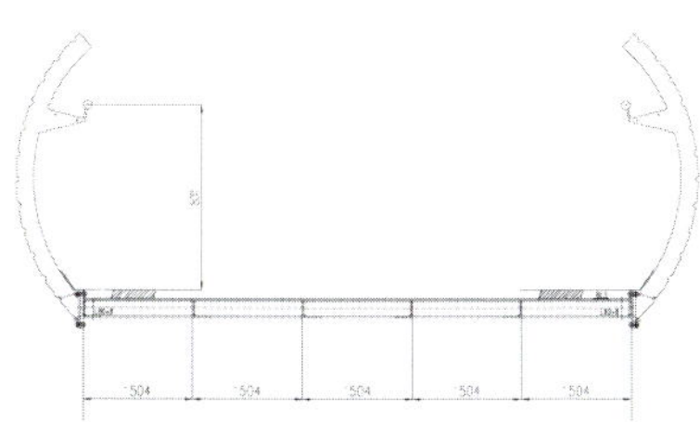

Cross Section of the Bridge

Beaver Lodge

A competition was organized in 1998 in the Swiss city of Bern to turn the Schwellenmätteli Restaurant, on the river Aar, into a new space for both locals and visitors. The competition sparked a debate about the various ways in which the area could be developed and the existing buildings could be renovated, refurbished, and preserved. (The area in question included a country house, places to sit shaded by trees, and a river restaurant.) Another discussion revolved around the suitability of interrupting the flow of the river to make way for new construction. Finally, one architectural team proposed building a restaurant as a barrier in the river, along the lines of a beaver dam, although the innovative design gives the impression that the structure is set within the wood itself, while the river runs unimpeded without any disturbance to the immediate surroundings. The river was therefore deemed out of bounds; moreover, no buildings belonging to the national heritage were destroyed. The result is a space in which the structure merges with its surroundings and visitors can revel in the tranquility, sunshine, luminosity, and flow of water.

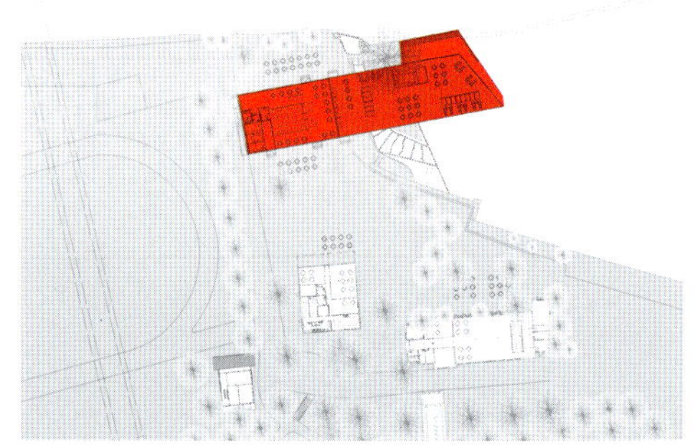

Site Plan

Client
Bern City Hall

Type of Project
Restaurant

Location
Bern, Switzerland

Total Surface Area
2,691 square feet (250 m^2)

Completion Date
2004

Photos ©
Dominique Uldry

Bern, Switzerland

River Restaurant

matti ragaz hitz architekten

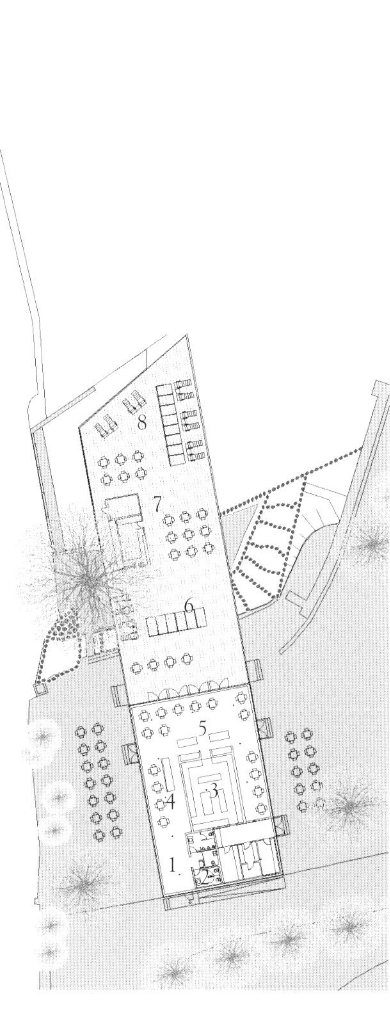

Plan

1- Entrance
2- Restrooms
3- Kitchen
4- Bar
5- Restaurant
6- Terrace
7- Outdoor Bar
8- Lounge Area

The Flussrestaurant Schwellenmätteli stands on top of the river and extends to one of its banks. The river can be seen at three different angles from the outdoor balconies, endowed with seats for enjoying the views. This 360-degree panorama takes in both the city of Bern and the natural landscapes around the restaurant, as well as the gentle flow of the water. An old country house forms part of the complex and offers multipurpose rooms for the use of visitors or for organized events. The restaurant's construction took advantage of the preexisting base of the river barrier, following the strategy of the beavers. Concrete was used for the foundations, steel for the supports, and wood for the roofs and floors.

Cross Section

Longitudinal Section

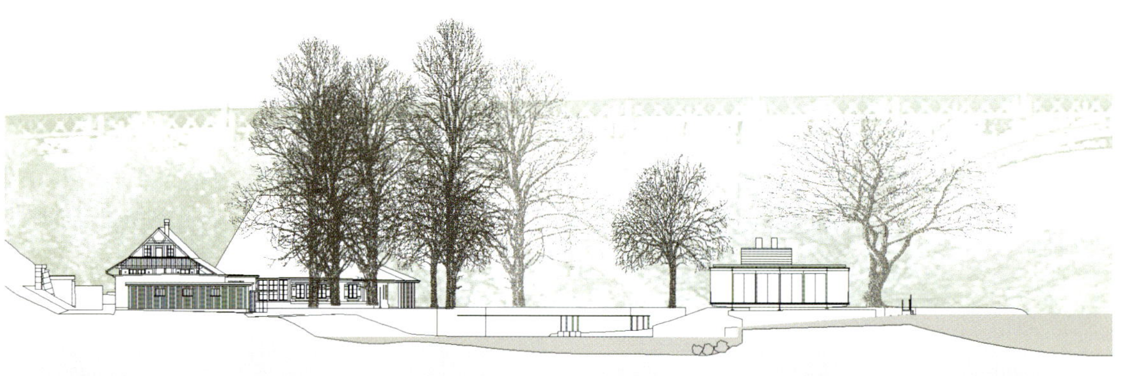

Cross Section

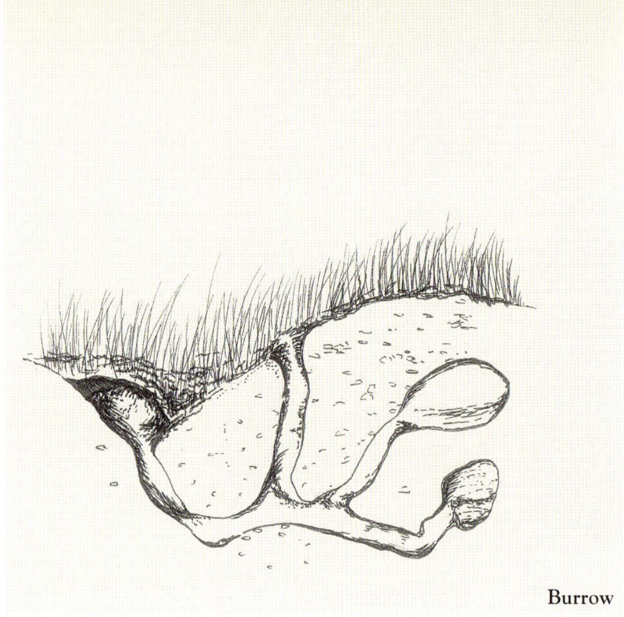

Burrow

The Portuguese Environmental Department declared the Gruta das Torres, caves in the municipality of Madalena do Pico, a national natural monument on account of its great geological value and its unrivaled dimensions on the Azores, with a height of up to 56 feet (17 m) and an extent of 3 miles (5 km.) The grotto opened to the public in 2005 with a new structure inside the main cave that serves as an information center for visitors. The entrance to the cave forms part of the visit's attractions because of the mysterious natural skylight that was formed as a result of the collapse of the roof and which has had a powerful impact on the landscape. The conservation of this skylight was of prime importance to the architectural team, which also had to take into account three other considerations vital to the development of the project: the risk of vandalism (the area is uninhabited), the very low budget, and the fact that the site is visited regularly only in summer. The team sought to combine the simplest possible form of protection for the natural skylight with the structure's design requirements. So, the building was endowed with a natural, wavy form, incorporating a stone wall 6 feet (1.8 m) high protecting the enormous entrance to the caves. Both the grotto and the building share the same material, albeit treated in different ways: the building's wall is made of mortar but the stone in the caves was used for the southern façade. This stone is now classified by UNESCO as part of humanity's landscape heritage.

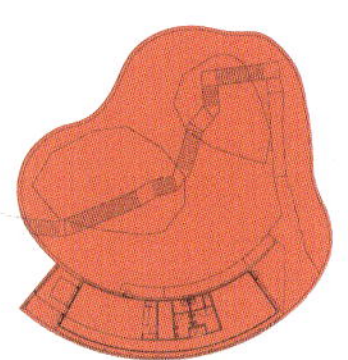

Site Plan

Client

Regional Government of the Azores

Type of Project

Information center

Location

Madalena do Pico, Portugal

Total Surface Area

2,476 square feet (230 m^2)

Completion Date

2005

Photos ©

Fernando Guerra + Sérgio Guerra

Madalena do Pico, Portugal

Gruta das Torres

SAMI.arquitectos

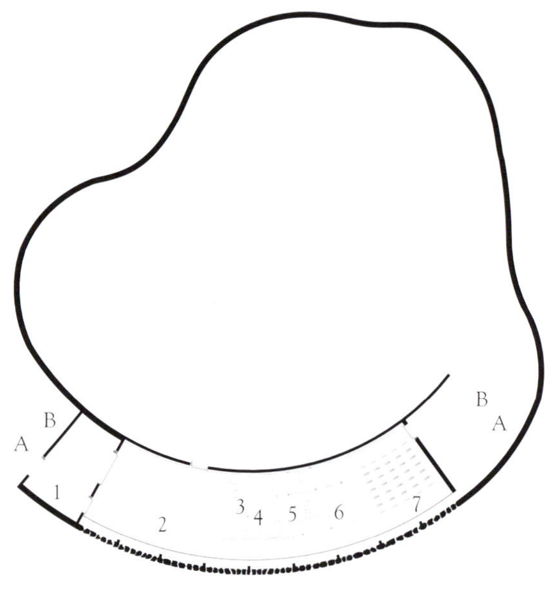

Plan

1- Entrance
2- Entrance Hall
3- Reception
4- Storage Area
5- Restrooms
6- Restrooms
7- Auditorium

The arrangement of the finely cut stone covering the walls allows light to penetrate the entire building while avoiding holes that could attract the attention of vandals. Apart from the stone wall, the building is covered with an impermeable layer of black that imitates the texture of the vitreous lava found in the deepest part of the cave. The building was constructed with reinforced concrete, resting on a furrow made of the same material to prevent any undesirable vibrations. Once visitors have crossed the threshold, they reach a patio formed by the transition in scale from the immensity of the landscape outside to the interior of the building. A stone staircase marks the path toward the center of the cave, which continues over a 131-foot (40-m) bridge that provides a short cut for a route otherwise measuring 1,312 feet (400 m).

The building, besides taking advantage of the slight natural slope of the land, is surrounded by lush vegetation and thereby merges with the landscape.

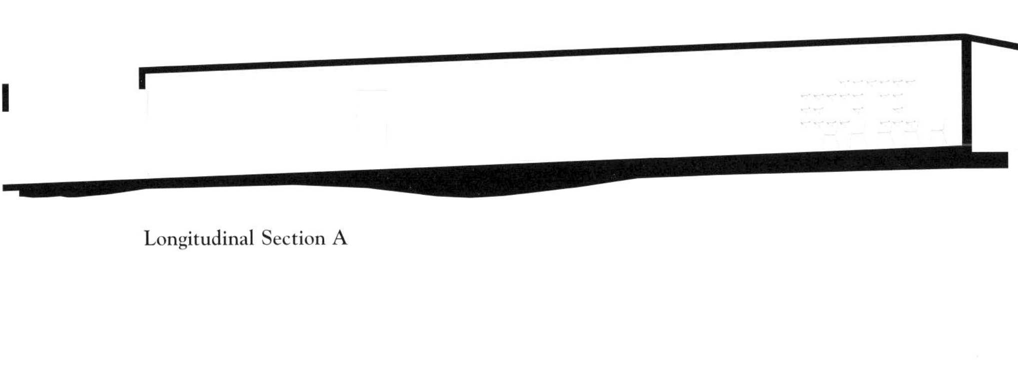

Longitudinal Section A

Longitudinal Section B

East Entrance

West Entrance

The relationship between the interior and the exterior is established by means of the stone cladding that covers the main building and creates openings of various sizes.

Beehive

Wasp Nest

Social Animal Constructive Structures

The conception of the organic world as a simple distribution of separate, autarchic living units bears absolutely no relation to reality. The benefits that can be gleaned from social constructive structures in terms of the exploitation of resources or protection from a hostile environment lead many animals, including human beings, to renounce living as isolated individuals. The organic world therefore contains a host of corporate amalgams that form a complex system of living relationships. Some of these organizations can involve sophisticated structures embracing up to millions of individuals, as in the case of some social insects. To guarantee the functionality and efficiency of these superorganisms, its members must be perfectly coordinated, be able to communicate (transfer information), and be specialized in performing specific functions. So, in complex animal organizations where there are not only queens and drones, but also specialists in construction (worker bees or ants), the resulting structures are strikingly different from those of other animals and arouse enormous interest from a sociobiological and constructive viewpoint.

Insects are the best-known social animals, but coral reefs and some birds provide other examples of complex communities capable of generating constructions of interest to us.

The interior of a beehive is made up of wax cells or panels in which the larvae grow and the community's food requirements are stored. The wax is secreted by worker bees nourished by the nectar and pollen of plants. They are responsible for building new cells as the queen lays eggs. The size of the cells will determine the sex and category of the bees that grow inside them, so the proportions of cells of different sizes are of vital importance to the community. The cells are made up of six rectangular sheets arranged in the form of a hexagonal prism, the base of which is closed not by a flat surface, but by three diamond shapes that constitute a type of flattened pyramid. The hexagonal format allows cells to be grouped together and takes full advantage of the available space. Worker bees use resin from trees to repair damage to the structure of the beehive.

A wasp nest is similar to a beehive in terms of the cells but not in those of the materials or shape. Wasps build their nest with a kind of cardboard that they make by massing together vegetal fibers with saliva; this material makes it possible to maintain a constant temperature inside. Wasp nests can be up to 20 inches (50 cm) long and are made up of downward-facing cells arranged in layers. As the cells

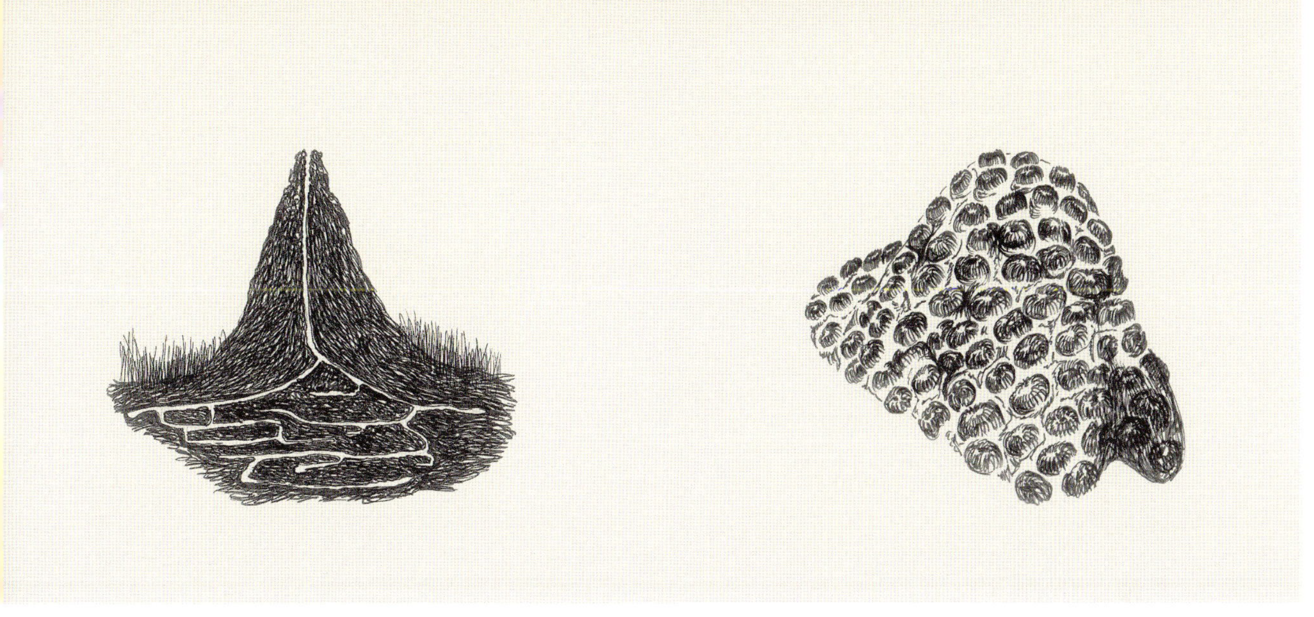

Termite Nest

Coral

increase in number, they fill up the space layer by layer, without any need to enlarge the cardboard covering around the nest, which is usually stuck to a wall or the branches of a tree.

In comparison with a beehive or wasp nest, an ant colony seems to be governed by confusion and mayhem, with a profusion of chambers joined together by means of complicated passageways containing—without any apparent order—larvae, eggs, and young ants, as well as food. Ants' bustling activity does not seem to follow any logic, but in fact it is underpinned by a complicated and finely tuned organization, based on the poles of individual freedom and an overriding sense of duty to the community. This explains the apparent anarchy—actually the sum total of individual initiatives.

Wilhelm Böche, in his work *Der Termiten Staat*, evaluates the effort made by termites in the construction of their nests in comparison with those of people when building human structures. If a man were to put up a building in the same proportions to his body as that of a termites' nest to a termite's body, it would soar up to the height of the Matterhorn (14,436 feet [4,400 m])! Their mounds of up to 23 feet (7 m) are not only remarkable for their height and shape, they are also astonishing for the efficacy of their systems for regulating the microclimate. Temperature is controlled by means of complicated ventilation systems, while carbon dioxide is also regulated. The nests are built on a north-south axis, to ensure minimum exposure of the surface during the hottest hours of the day and maximum capture of light and heat at dawn and nightfall. The water-gathering system consists of galleries up to 131 feet (40 m) deep that extract water from the phreatic stratum.

Corals are elemental creatures that live in large colonies to make up for structural deficiencies. In order to encourage individual specialization, there must be fluid intercommunication, and this is achieved via a tube with fleshy walls, the coenosarc, which constitutes the backbone of the colony. The components of the colony establish themselves on the coenosarc, surrounded by a chitinous crown, the hydrotheca, into which the animal can retreat in case of danger.

Beehive

The Beehive in the industrial hub of Culver City, California, is an innovative office building and conference center that also serves as the façade for three factory warehouses. The client wanted a flexible building that would bestow a new architectural identity on this area, which only ten years ago was considered little more than a remote, anonymous outpost of Los Angeles. The building was conceived as a two-story volume with extensive, open-plan work areas, and it had to adapt to the characteristics of the site, which were largely defined by the adjacent buildings. The Beehive, whose name refers to its source of conceptual inspiration, consists of a layered structure in which each piece seems to have been added at a different time, each according to its own separate logic. However, as in the case of actual beehives, every piece has its own specific function and is essential to the overall harmony. The surrounding area is divided among three sections of buildings that leave only 35 feet (10 m) free for the façade. The new building replaced an old wooden structure, although it has retained its original dimensions. The architects came up with a distinctive, efficient strategy capable of connecting the outdoor public space with the interior of the building in a functional manner, while also creating a bold, sculptural image.

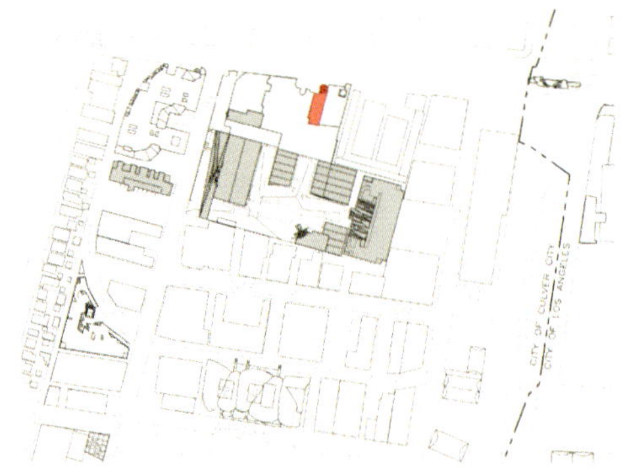

Site Plan

Client

Frederick and Laurie Samitaur Smith

Type of Project

Offices and conference center

Location

Culver City, California

Total surface area

9,903 square feet (920 m²)

Completion Date

2001

Photos ©

Tom Bonner Photography

Culver City, California

Beehive

Eric Owen Moss Architects

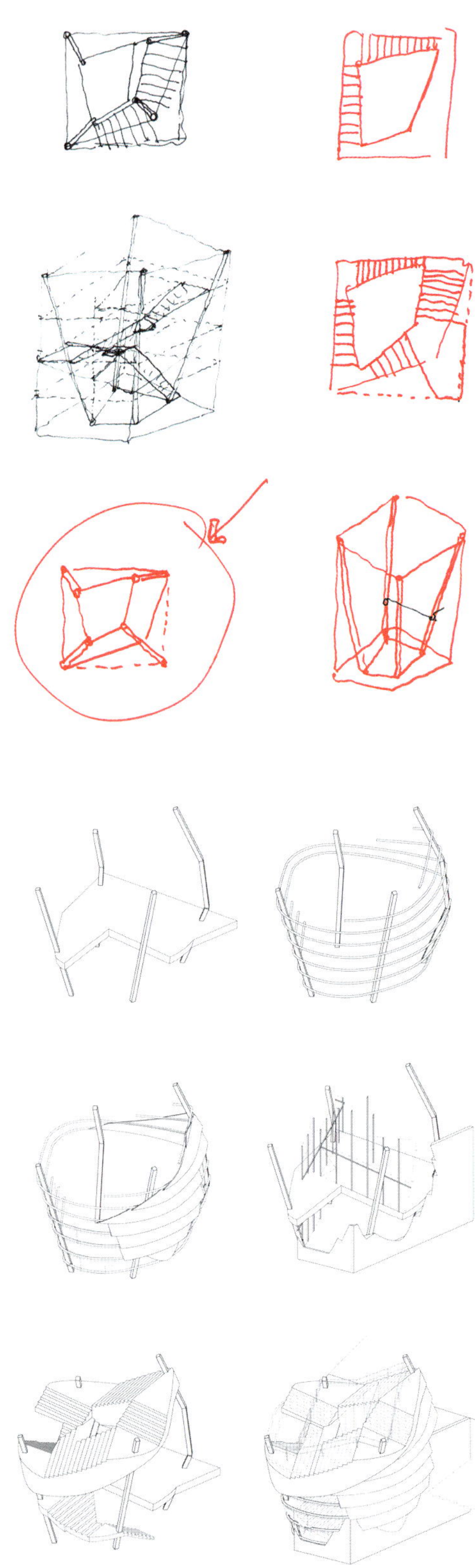

Preliminary Sketches

The ground floor contains the reception and the main entrance to the offices. The visitor, once inside, faces a staircase leading to the first floor, which contains the conference room, while a second staircase in the form of a triangle rises around the pyramidal skylight that constitutes the roof of the Beehive. This roof, which also serves as a large terrace for more informal meetings, provides expansive views of the city. The placement of the building ensures that natural light not only pours through the central skylight and side windows but also penetrates down to the ground floor. The front part of the building is directly linked to its rear section on both levels.

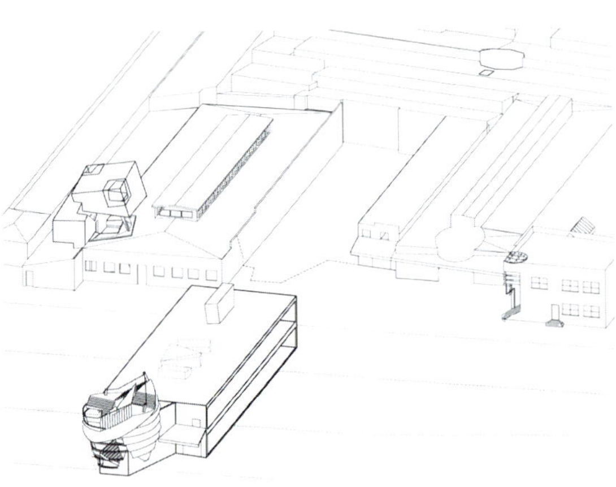

General axonometric

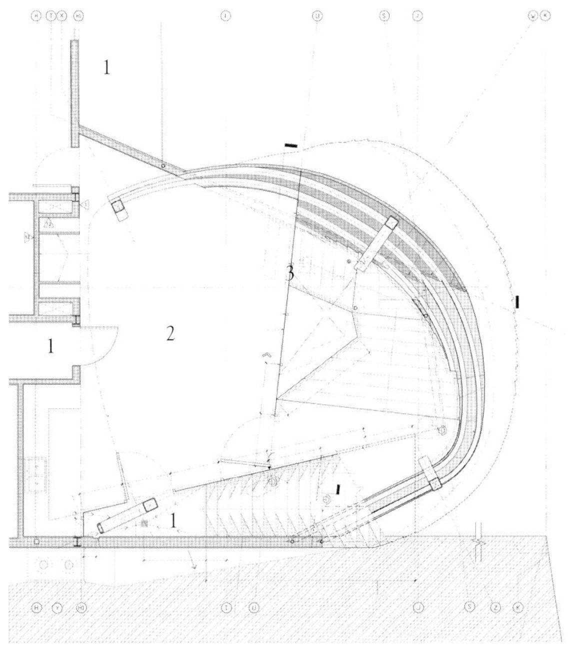

Second Floor

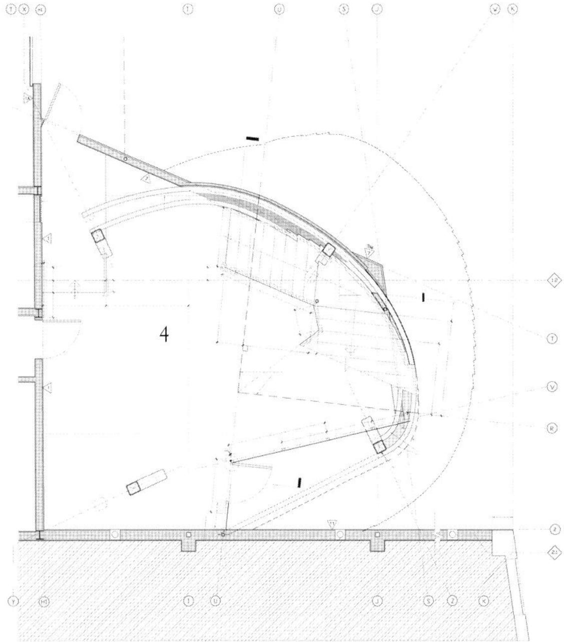

Ground Floor

1- Entrance
2- Reception
3- Staircase
4- Conference Room

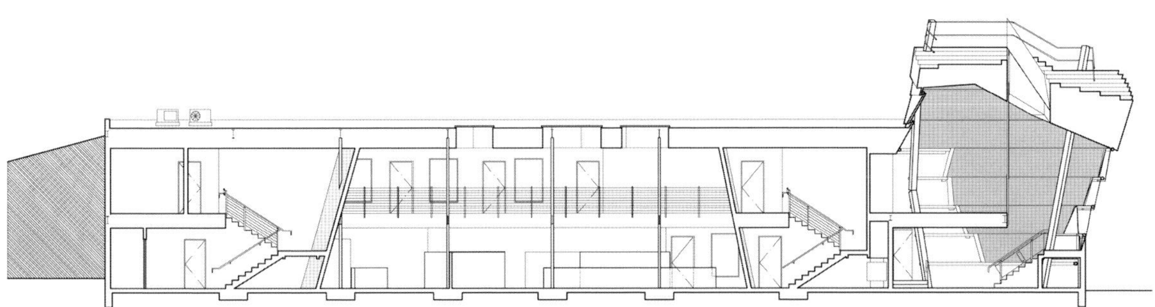

General Longitudinal Section

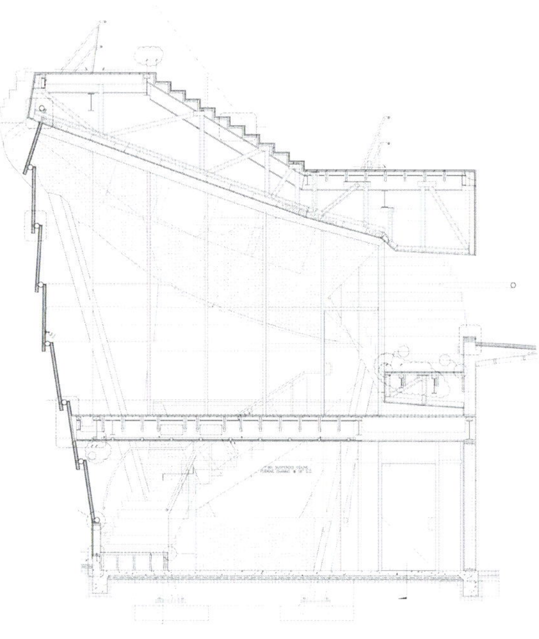

Cross Section

The building's structure is supported by four steel columns capable of being bent or inclined independently of one other. Some thinner curved beams run along the entire length of the building to connect the four columns at the base and thus endow the structure with a continuous system. The skin of the building is a shingle system of metal glass planes and thin sheet-metal walls that is expressed on both the interior and exterior. When seen from the street, the Beehive and its adjacent buildings create a kind of interior square.

The enigmatic exterior appearance of this extension was achieved by means of the double façade cladding the volume, which also serves as heat insulation for the interior space.

Beehive

This project won a competition organized in 2006 by the Slovenian Housing Fund, a government program to promote low-cost housing for young families. The winning proposal was chosen for its financial and functional approach, and above all for the ingenious exploitation of the inhabitable space and the flexibility of its design. The two blocks, each measuring 197 by 92 feet (60 by 28 m), face Izola Bay, with a chain of mountains to the rear. Both blocks contain thirty apartments of various sizes, ranging from small studios to three-bedroom apartments. The latter have no structural elements inside, to make the arrangement and organization as flexible as possible. The architects were inspired by the form of beehives, allowing them to merge the buildings into the setting and establish a close, harmonious relationship with the Mediterranean climate and an optimal balance between light and shade—vital factors for this type of housing.

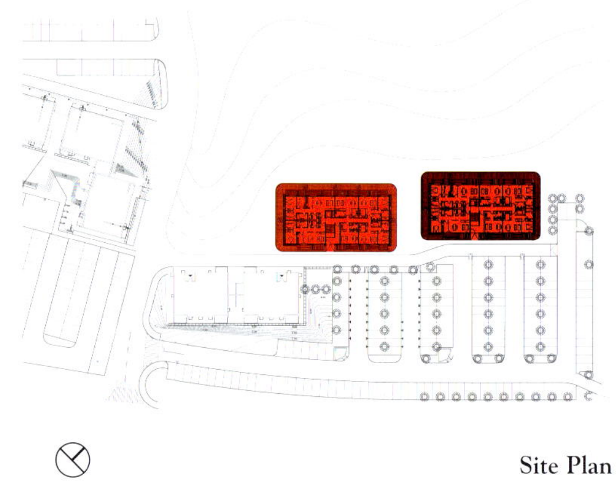
Site Plan

Client
Slovenian Housing Fund and Izola City Hall

Type of Project
Apartment building

Location
Izola, Slovenia

Total Surface Area
58,685 square feet (5,452 m^2)

Completion Date
2006

Photos ©
Tomaz Gregorc

Izola, Slovenia

Izola Apartments

OFIS arhitekti

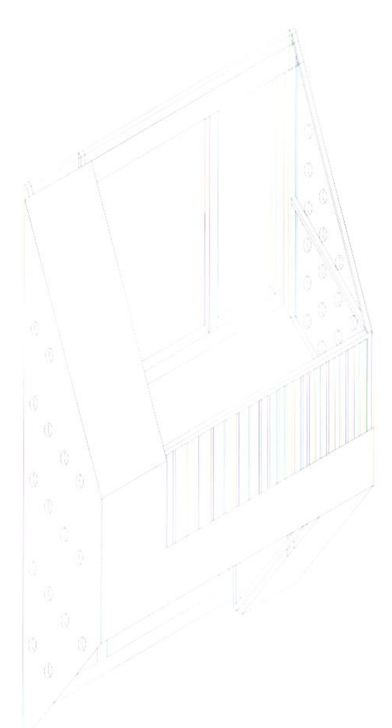

Axonometric View of the Balcony

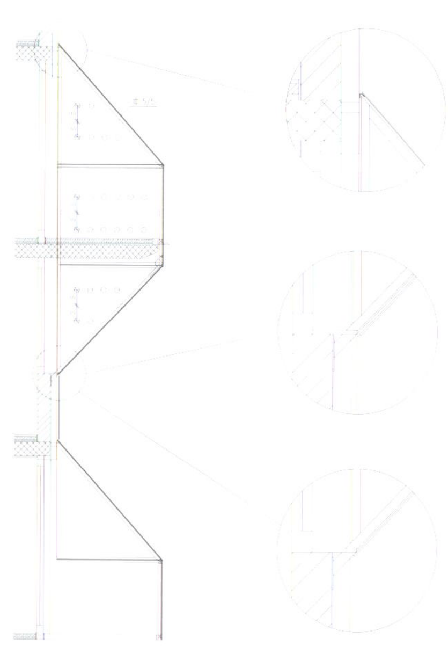

Construction Details of the Balcony

Each home is fitted with a balcony that serves to connect the interior with the exterior, as well as enhancing natural ventilation and lighting. A transparent fabric covering the balcony sets up an intimate atmosphere while still permitting the occupants to enjoy a view of the bay from indoors. The fabric also forms shadows that further link the interior with the exterior, thereby making the rooms look bigger. Perforated panels along the sides of each apartment enable the summer breeze to waft through the living space. The lower section of each balcony has a space that has been left free for air-conditioning units. The use of strong, bright colors was intended to create a different atmosphere in each of the apartments.

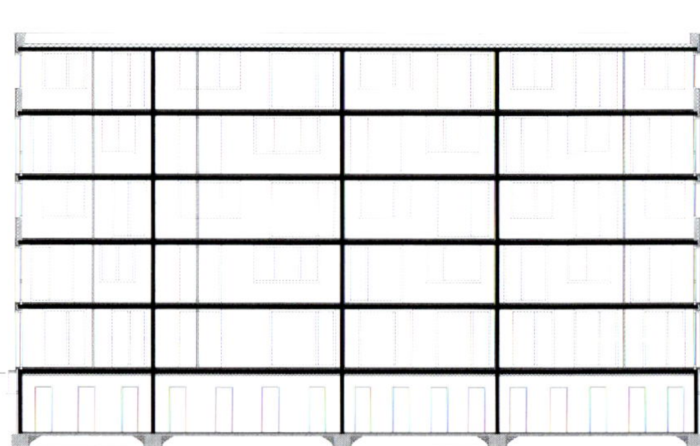

Longitudinal Section

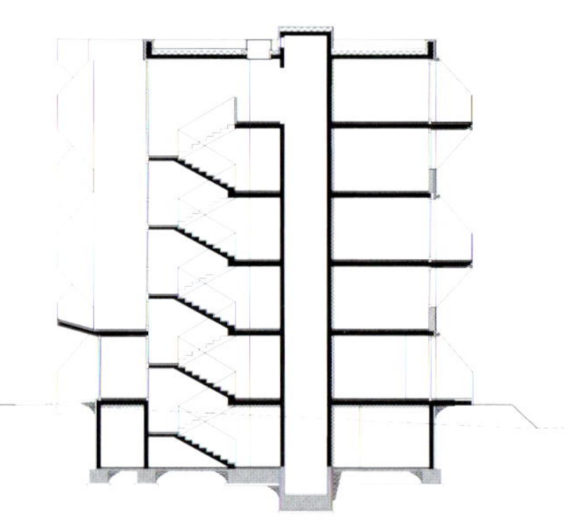

Cross Section

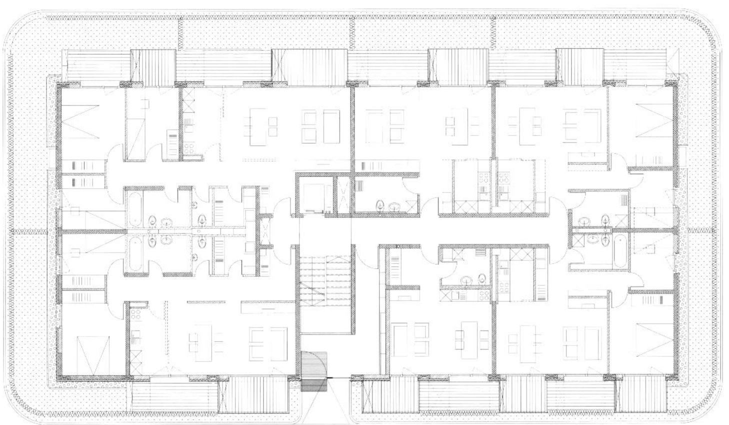

Ground Floor

Plan

South Elevation

North Elevation

East Elevation

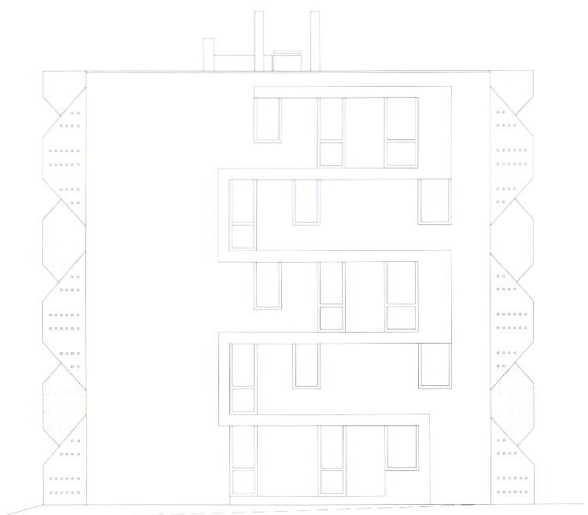

West Elevation

The color scheme chosen for the various elements making up the façade further emphasizes the analogy with a beehive.

Beehive

A beekeeper working in an area just south of Cashiers, North Carolina, needed two new buildings for making honey: first, an apiary for processing and storing the honey taken from his hives and, second, a space to serve as an exclusive sales point and occasional open-air work area. The apiary was conceived as a single workspace, divided into two separate areas with steel containers, equipment for processing honey, and shelves to display the produce for sale to the public. Its distinguishing architectural elements are a steel sheet and an angular glass wall, facing southeast, to allow light to filter into the workspace. In order to protect the treated honey, the structure is raised from the ground, thereby also allowing the residues of the processing to be drained uninterruptedly. The design was inspired by the domestic maintenance methods and behavior of bees. This modern apiary consists of a four-sided beehive, organized into a series of octagonal frames that articulate and separate the cells of the honeycomb in the lower part of the beehive. The mobile frames make it possible to remove the stored honey without disturbing or damaging the cells of the honeycomb.

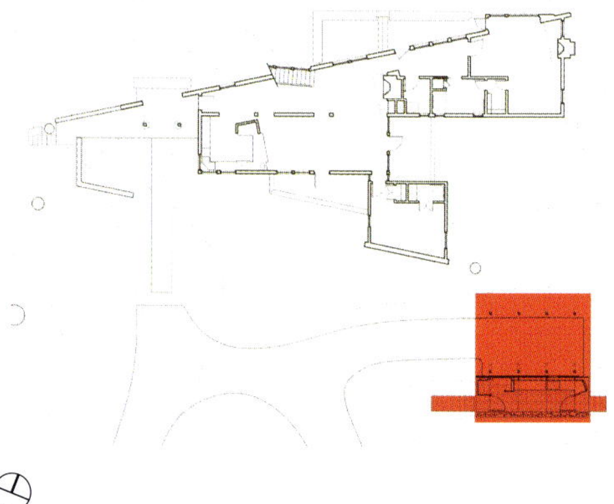

Site Plan

Client
Leslie and Craig Moore

Type of Project
Apiary and display

Location
Cashiers, North Carolina

Total Surface Area
194 square feet (18 m^2)

Completion Date
1998

Photos ©
Richard Johnson

Cashiers, North Carolina

Moore Apiary

Marlon Blackwell

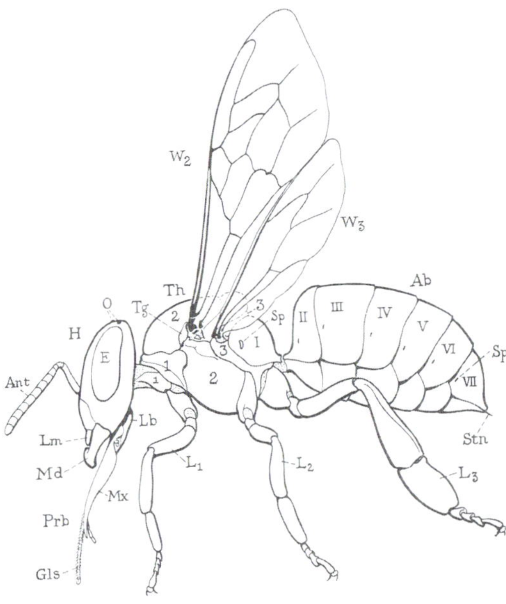

Diagram of a Bee

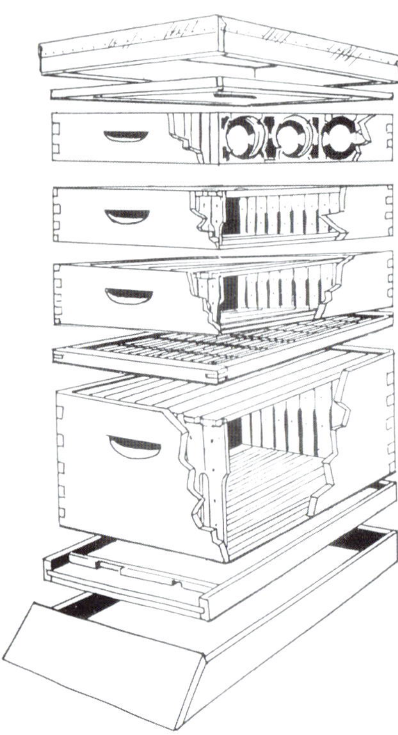

Diagram of a Honey Box

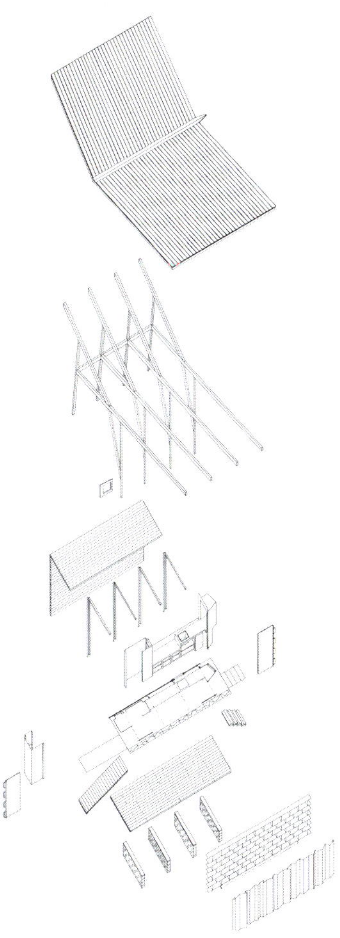

Exploded Axonometric

A series of glass panels are configured in horizontal layers, and the glass acts as a continuous membrane while also serving as shelves for the finished honey jars. The intersection of the two spaces—dominated by steel and glass, respectively—produces effects of transparency, translucence, and opacity in the window, depending on the season and the time of day. The construction's dense polyrhythmic nature establishes a vivid dynamism as it embraces the area's climatic variations, the living organic forms around the apiary and the activity within it. The intense interrelationship between the beekeeper's equipment and the bee's capacity to adapt to this equipment is crucial to the continuous production of honey and the survival of the bee colony.

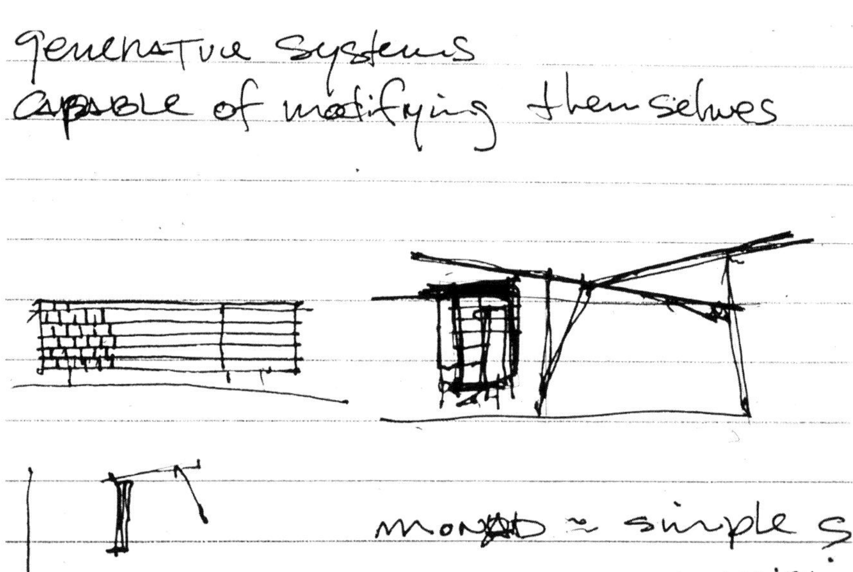

Preliminary Sketch

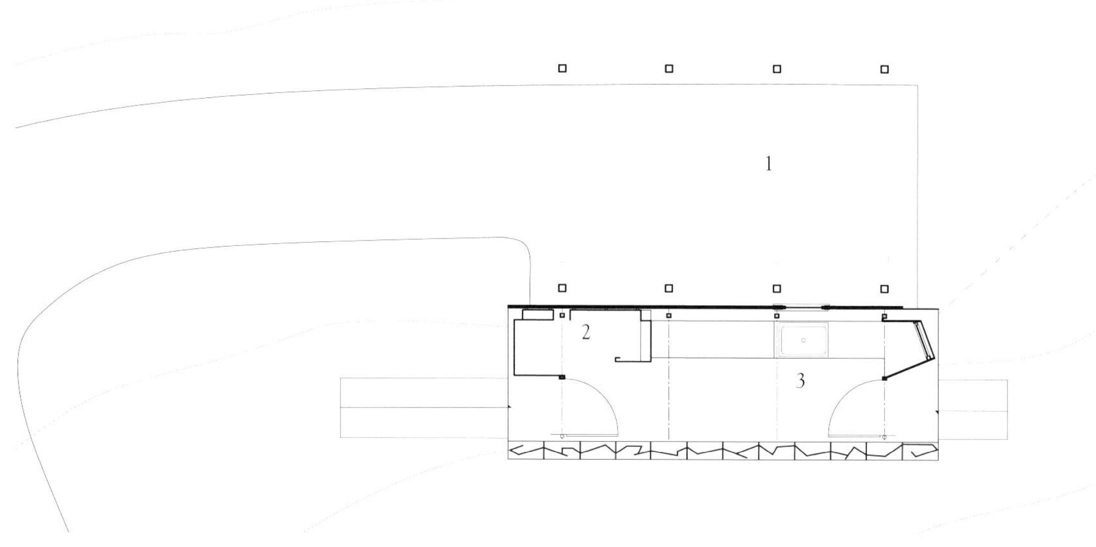

General Plan

1- Parking Lot
2- Tool Storage Area
3- Work Area

The apiary is a volumetric response to the confluence of natural, rational processes, as it combines various elements and functions within a single workspace. The overall structure is linked to four pieces of concrete. A wing of the inverted metal roof serves as a counterpoint to the other forms, marking out its independence while also establishing a complementary relationship with the apiary. Both structures are made of interlocking veneered wood and steel tubes, which were left to rust for nine months, along with the other steel elements, before being sealed with a sturdy varnish. Part of the steel structure was made in Arkansas and then assembled in situ—a procedure that lasted an entire month.

Termite Nest

This project formed part of the Royal Botanic Gardens in Kew, long considered one of London's most emblematic parks on account of its famous greenhouses and declared a UNESCO World Heritage Site in 2003. The management required a new greenhouse for its revitalized collection of alpine plants, often thought of as the "lost gem" of Kew Gardens. The main aim was to boost the profile of this collection by providing a new focal point in this part of the gardens' grounds, in addition to ensuring that the building's new location should have a minimal impact on the existing plants and that there should be a smooth transition between the interior and the outdoor environment. The structure allows suitable amounts of natural light to penetrate inside, as well as providing optimum cooling conditions and a constant circulation of air. Improved access was another key feature of the design, as the structure is endowed with entrances at both ends of the building, each with its own foyer, thereby guaranteeing fluid circulation of the public. The architects drew inspiration from the design of termite nests, particularly in terms of the refrigeration system, and even reproduced their shape, which proves ideal for creating conditions suited to the smooth adaptation of new plants.

Site Plan

Client
Royal Botanic Gardens, Kew

Type of Project
Cultural facility

Location
London, England

Total Surface Area
3,853 square feet (358 m²)

Completion date
2005

Photos ©
Dennis Gilbert/VIEW, Nick Guttridge/VIEW

London, England

Davies Alpine Greenhouse

Wilkinson Eyre Architects

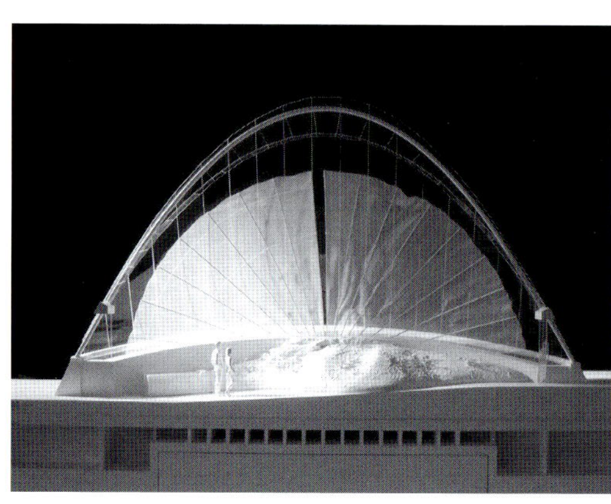

Unfolding of the Sunscreen

The structure is distinguished by twin arches, each of sufficient height to prevent plants from overheating. The stainless-steel bars running from the bottom to the top of each arch serve as struts for the entire structure, and they have been painted an aluminum color to enhance the reflection of sunlight. An excellent refrigeration system was created with the semicylindrical form of the glass arches and the maze of small concrete walls embedded in the basement floor. Cold air circulates around the entire perimeter of the greenhouse, thanks to the concrete maze, while the curved surfaces of the façades allow hot air to be released easily. The north-south orientation seeks to minimize exposure to solar radiation, while a screen in the form of a peacock's tail, unfolded according to the time of the year, casts a shadow within the building itself.

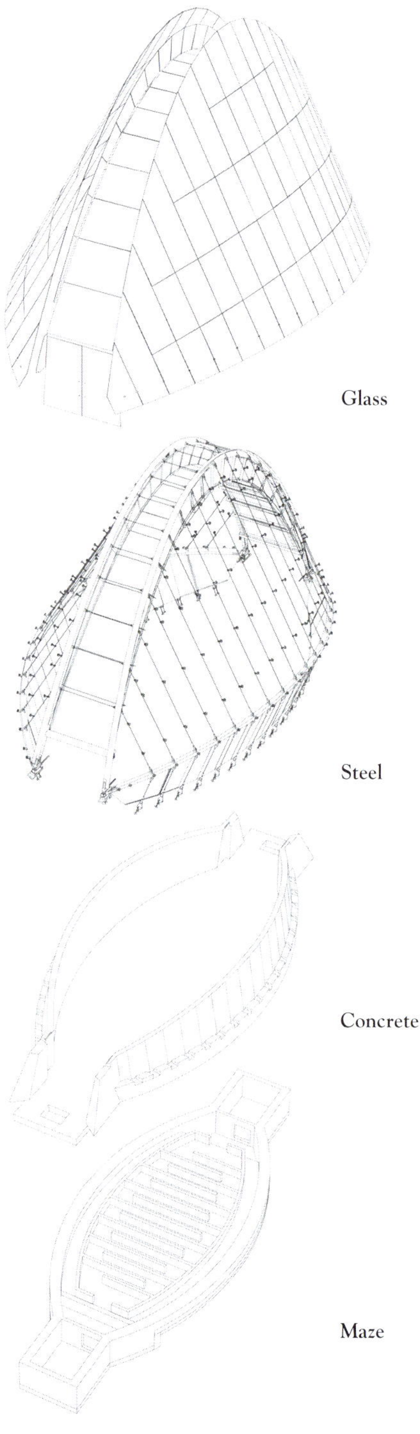

Axonometric Views of the Structure

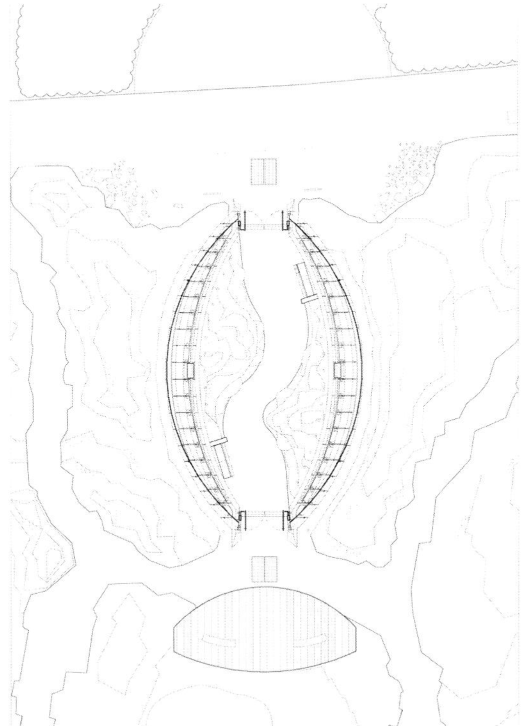

Ground Floor

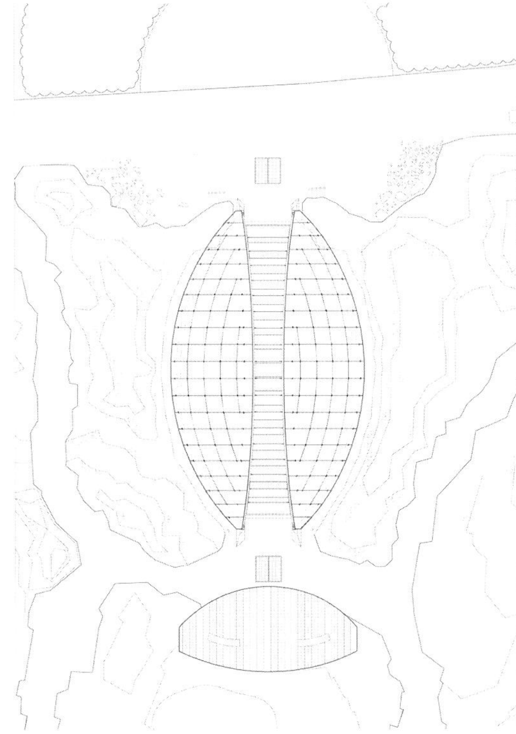

Plan of the Roof

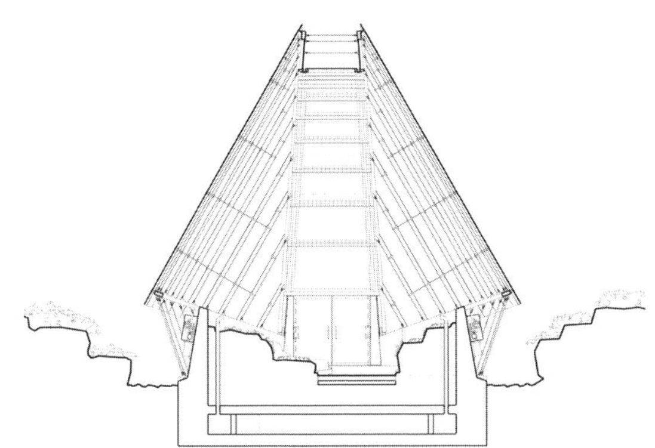

Cross Section

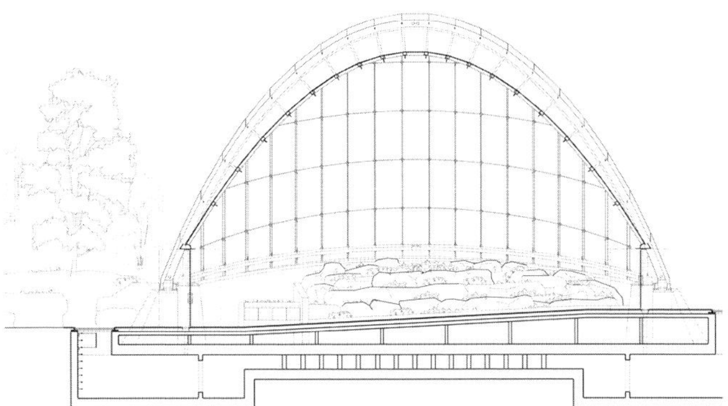

Longitudinal Section

Detail of the Structure

Axonometric Views of the Structure

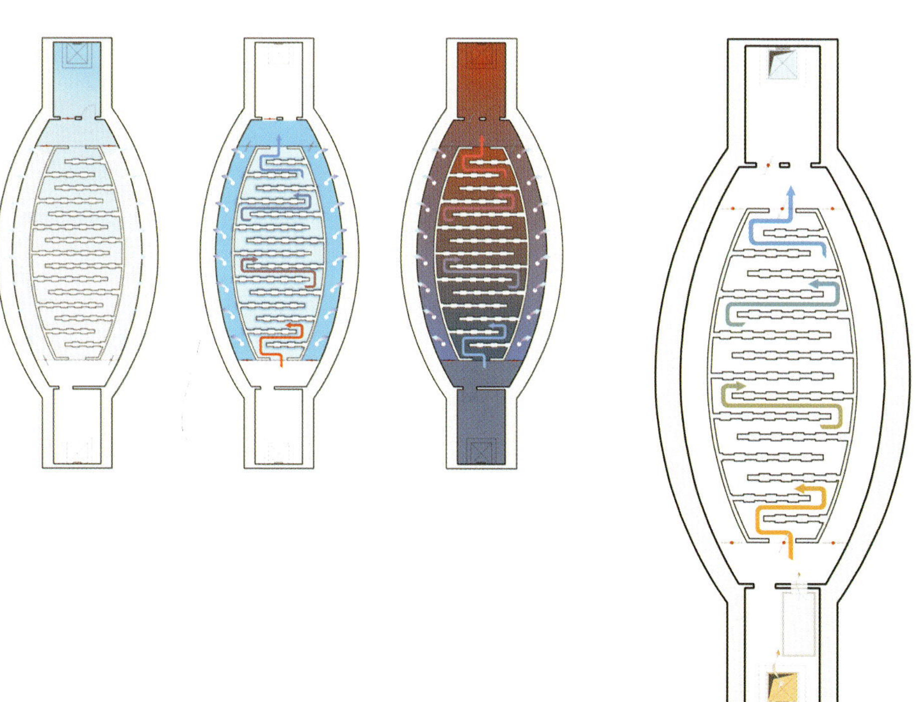

Maze System in the Basement

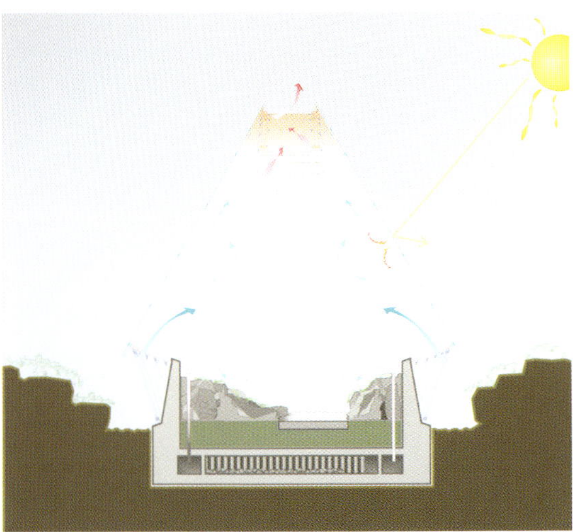

Study of the Natural Cooling System

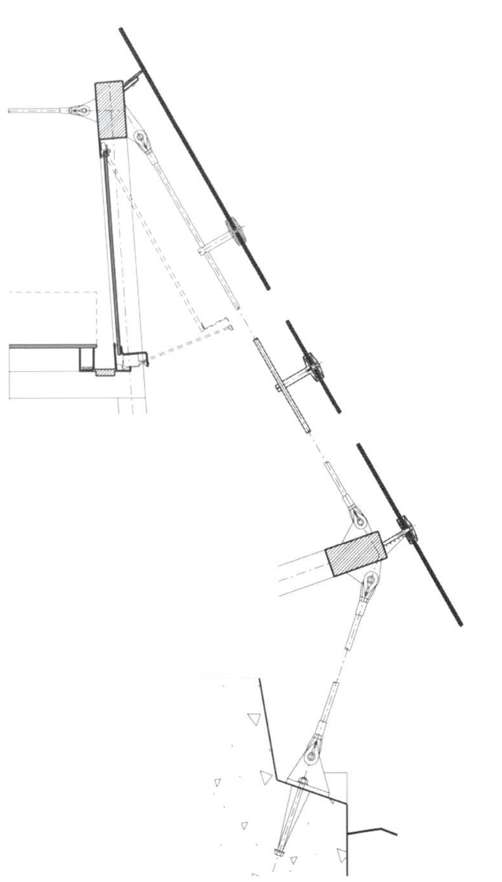

Construction Detail

Termite Nest

The Hysteric Ballroom was the winning project in an architecture competition held in Almere, Holland, in 2006. The idea was to come up with a simple solution that combined compactness with a large surface area for a house in the middle of a wood. The design echoed the remote wilderness of nature to create a closed structure, integrated into the wood, that was inspired by termite nests. Technological advances in construction made it possible to allow the internal points to rotate inside the structure while the roofs and walls remained completely accessible. Furthermore, two spheres and two spirals were integrated into the construction to act as cushioning, and this increased the usable surface area by 40 percent. This strategy meant that a single space could be used to maximum advantage or be modified as required, without the occupants having to leave the house at all. The furniture is adapted to the functional needs of the moment, as it is integrated into the interior of the space by being attached to the structure's floors, walls, and roofs. Each room can therefore change its use as the spheres and spirals rotate. While this rotation occurs, various landscapes, forms, and lighting configurations can be perceived, and these spirals also act as dividing walls, isolating each room without any need to install doors.

Site Plan

Client
Public competition

Type of Project
House

Location
Almere, The Netherlands

Total Surface Area
667 square feet (62 m^2)

Completion Date
2007

Renders ©
bube architects

Almere, The Netherlands

Hysteric Ballroom

bube architects

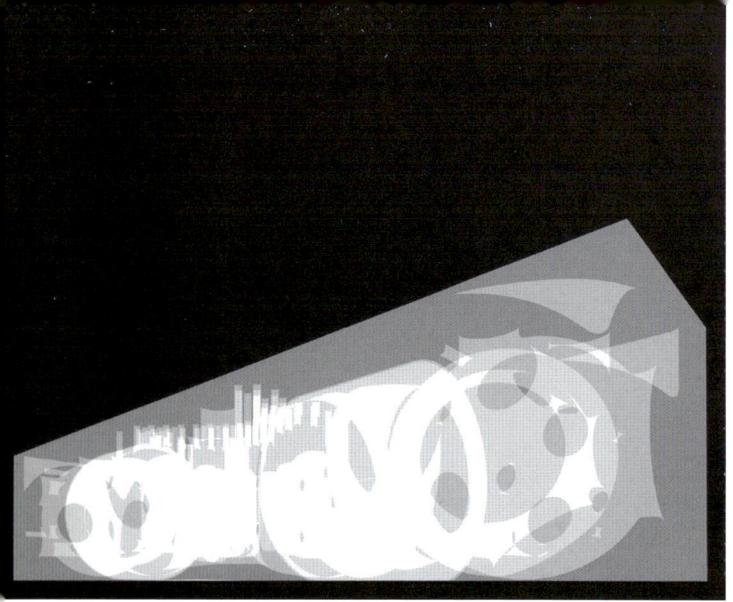

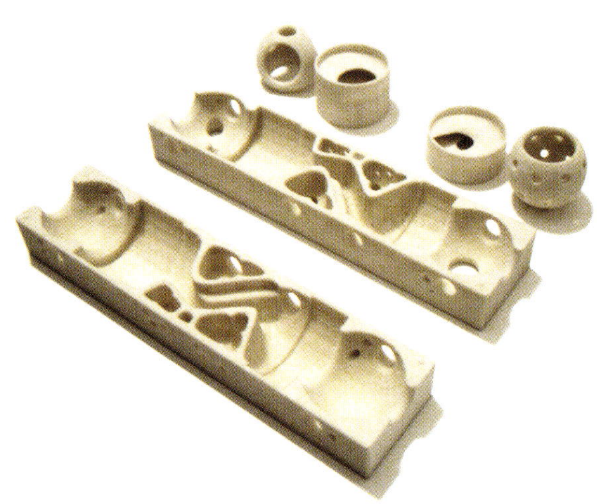

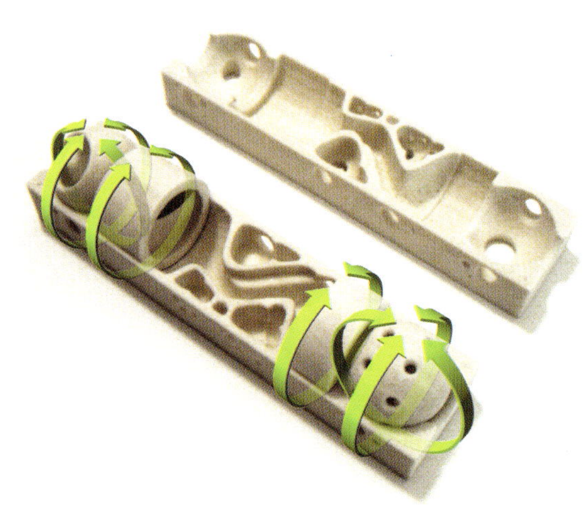

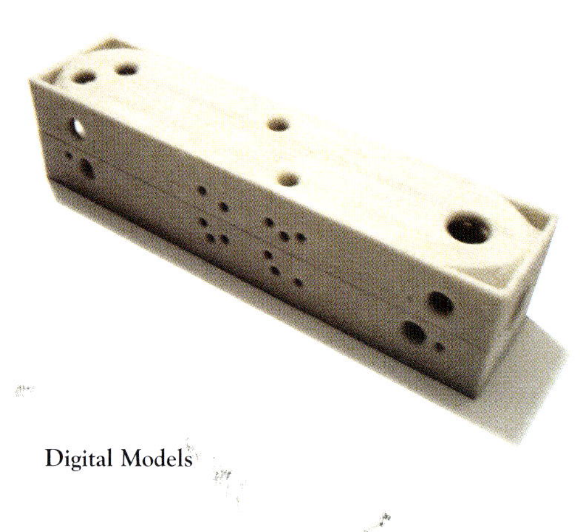

Digital Models

The final design was decided upon after creating prototypes that made it possible to achieve maximum precision in the movement of the revolving parts. These were built by using a totally computerized machine that cut them out of polystyrene before covering them with glass fiber and epoxy resin. The result is a light, completely insulated house that challenges the concept of displacement and organization of interior space while offering an alternative form of living by maximizing the use of the space. As often happens with projects of this scope, various explicit solutions were sought through a clear reciprocity between design and setting, based on a mixture of intuition and research on the part of the architects.

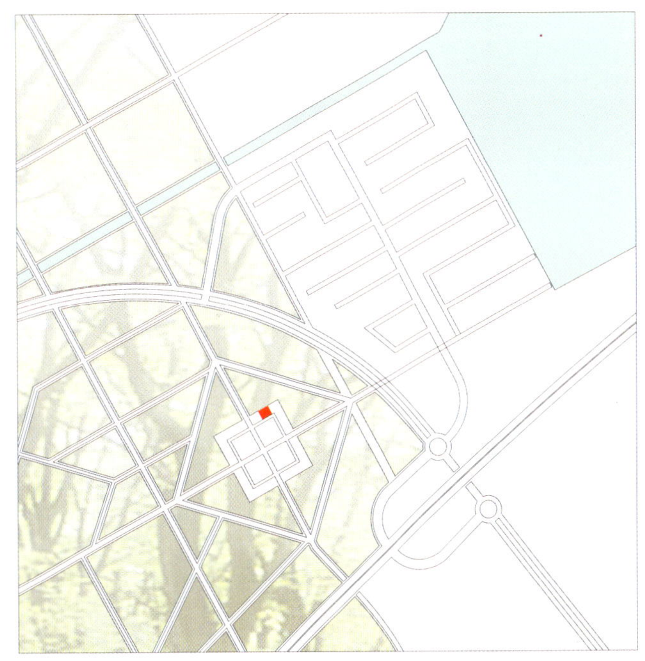

Site Plan

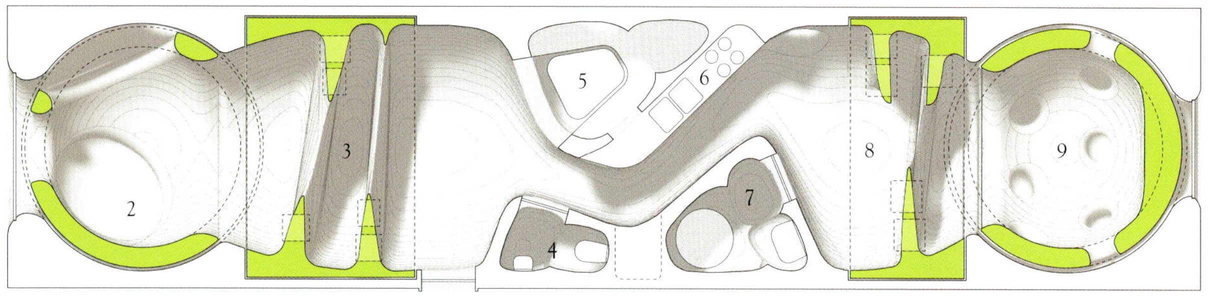

Plan

1- Entrance
2- Living Room
3- Library
4- Toilet
5- Sitting Area
6- Kitchen
7- Bathroom
8- Closet
9- Bedroom

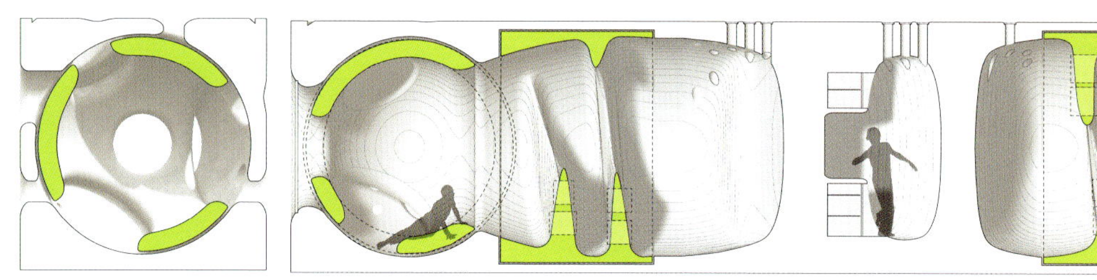

Cross Section

Longitudinal Section

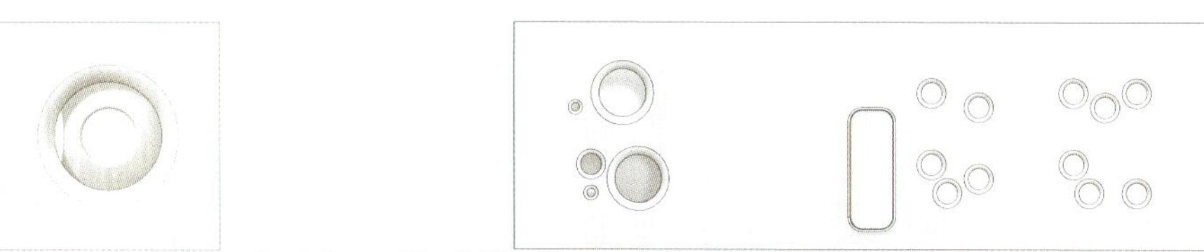

Front Elevation

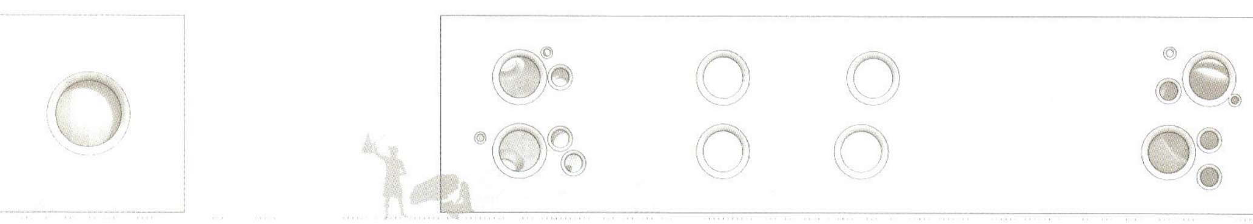

Side Elevations

Rear Elevation

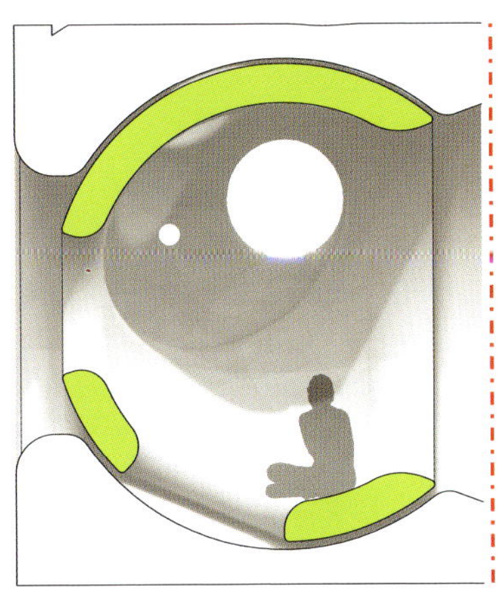
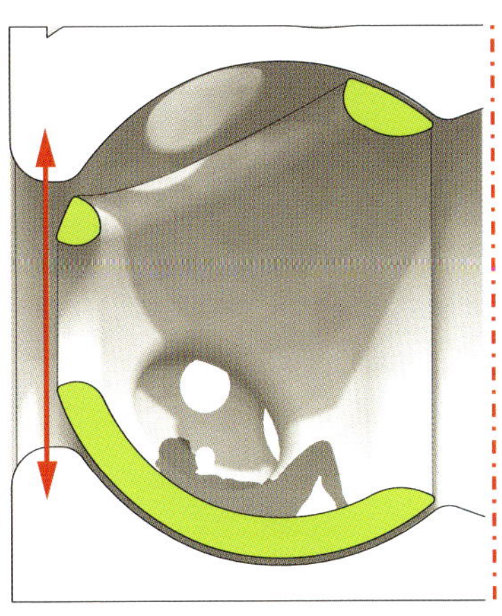

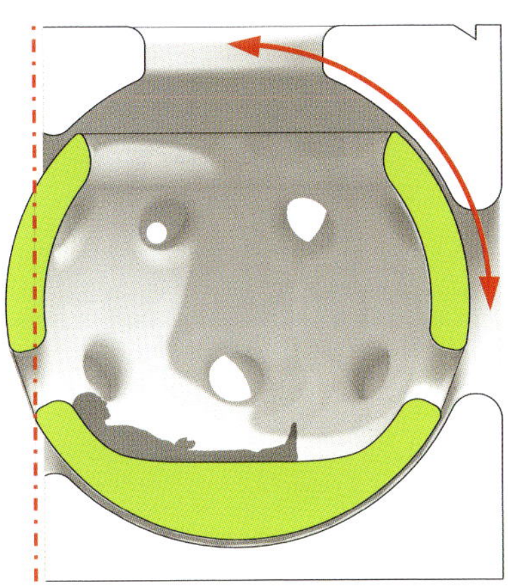
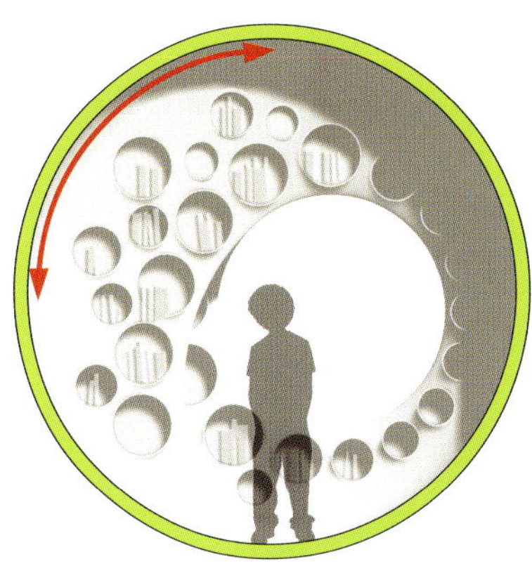

Diagrams of the Various Configurations of the Interior Space

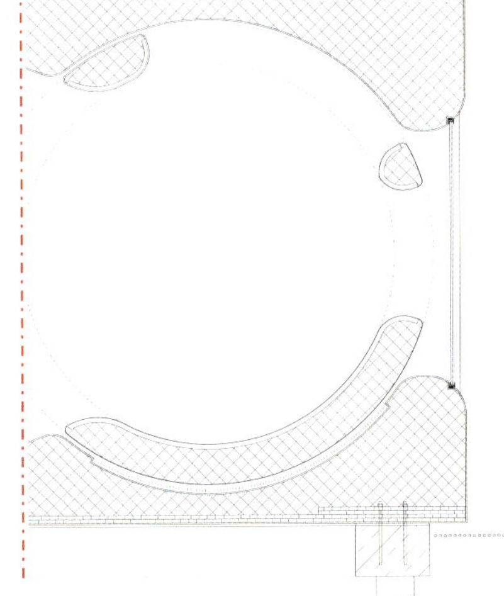

Construction Detail

A single space is transformed from a living room into a bedroom when its inhabitants make the structure rotate through movements within the house.

Coral

Apart from being an underwater spa, Coral City Island is a pioneer of wellness with a new natural dimension. It is also an attractive and distinctive cultural center offering a wide range of events, adventures, and experiences of all kinds. The basic purpose of Coral City Island is scientific research and regeneration of the marine ecosystem, but the need for financial self-sufficiency led it to promote itself as a tourist attraction and it now receives visitors from all over the world. This project involves the creation of a large marine research laboratory in Dubai that would be capable of planning and predicting the ecological changes caused by future construction in the Gulf. Half the structure lies underwater and reproduces the strategy of a coral reef by covering a wide range of functions in a single space. The project stirs the memories of a recent past when the inhabitants of Dubai lived off the fruits of the sea and corals still formed part of the marine ecosystem, before being completely destroyed by unbridled exploitation. The underwater areas allow visitors to relax and explore a regenerated natural setting that will breathe new life into the city, which is now predominantly focused on industry, tourism, and commerce.

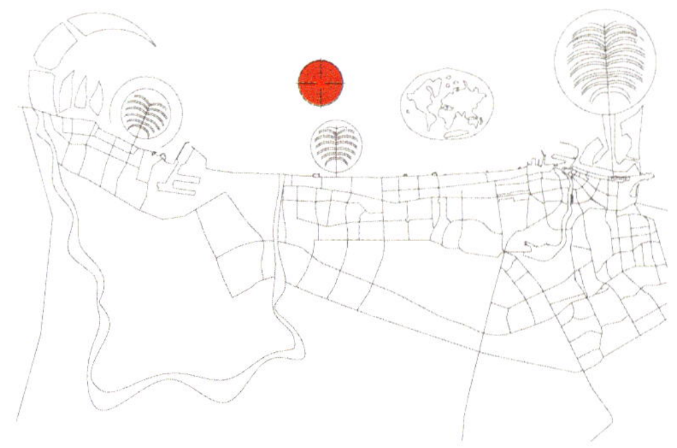

Site Plan

Client

Architectural Association
Technical Studies Exhibition

Type of Project

Spa and scientific research center

Location

Dubai, United Arab Emirates

Total Surface Area

136,486 square feet (12,680 m^2)

Completion Date

2007 (unbuilt project)

Renders ©

Damian Figueras

Dubai, United Arab Emirates

Coral City Island

Damian Figueras

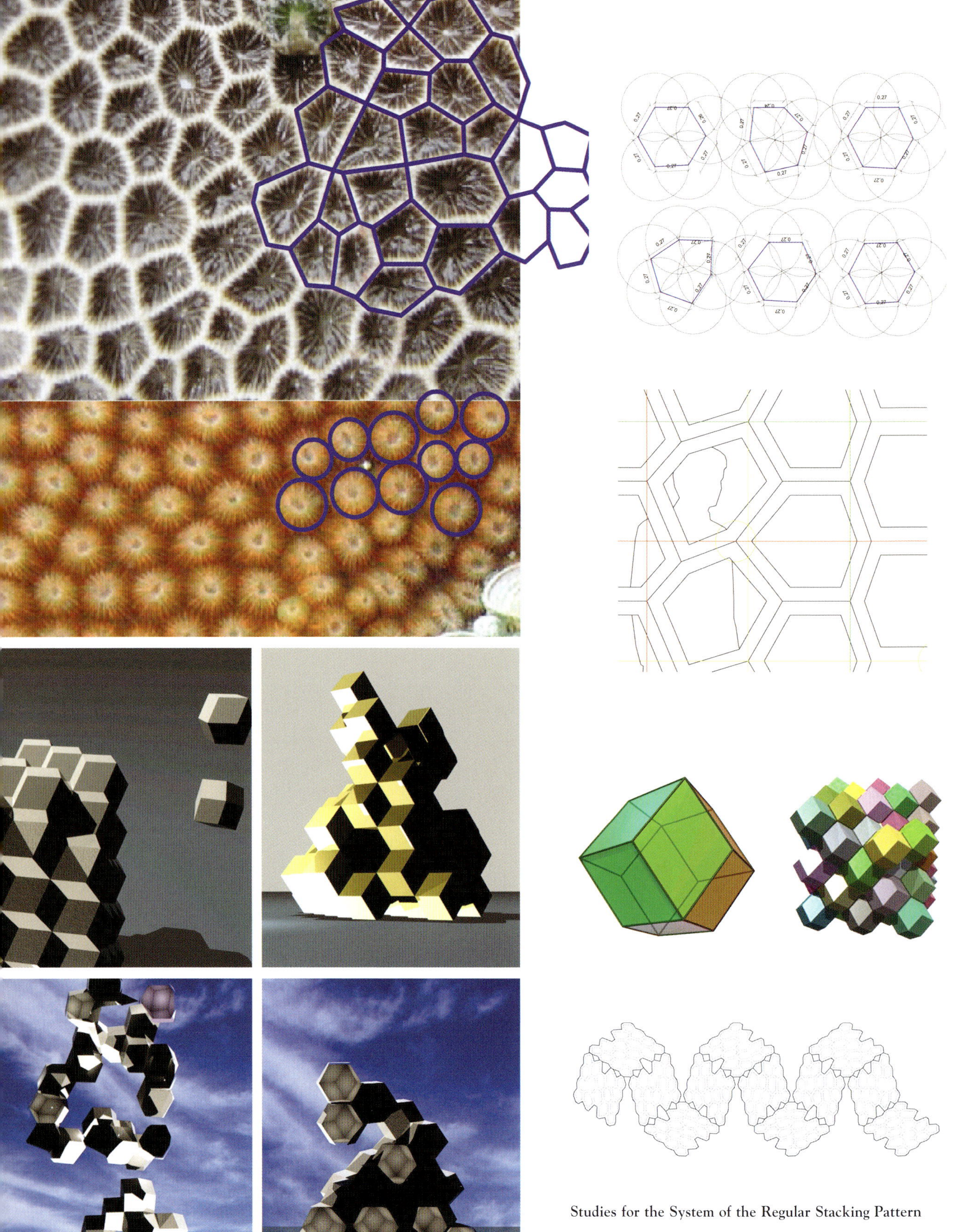

Studies for the System of the Regular Stacking Pattern

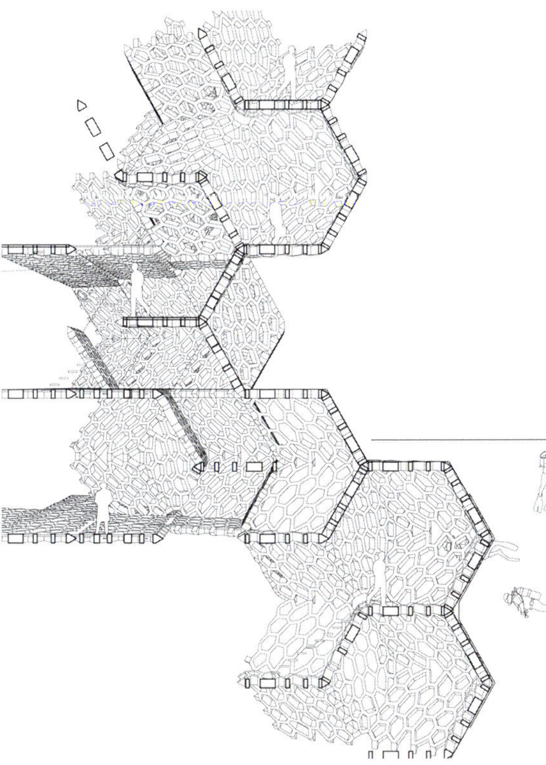

Partial Section in Perspective

The architect drew inspiration from the design techniques of coral reefs, which have proved effective for thousands of years within their ecosystems. Coral reefs are not so far removed from urban settlements, in the sense that they provide a shelter for everyday vital functions. The structure of a coral, resembling the branches of a tree or the antlers of a stag, seeks to maximize the surface area exposed to the elements, thereby allowing natural light to pour into the various spaces and cross ventilation to pass through from all directions. Furthermore, the oval shape of the coral brain provides a more concentrated, protected space that served as an analogy for the design of the laboratory. The coral star, in its turn, offers the possibility of a living skin that covers the structure and enhances the interaction with the environment and its climatic conditions.

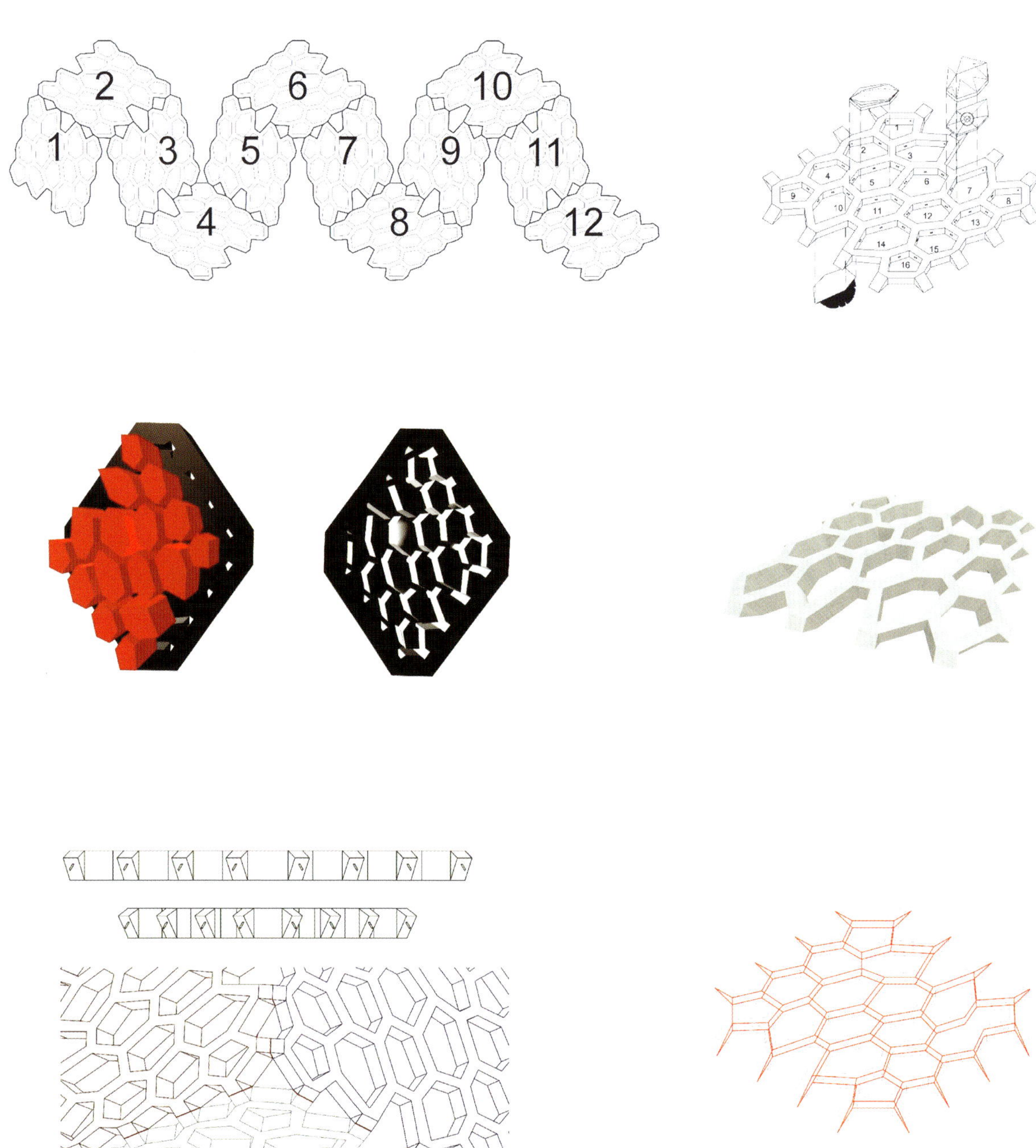

Studies for the Design of Prefabricated Panels for the Cladding

A reef sometimes forms on top of old corals that wither into rocky skeletons when they die, before being broken down into fine sand that then hardens and serves as a foundation for new coral structures. The end results of this process are limestone structures renowned for attracting natural life of great ecological diversity. The project was inspired by this principle to connect the building's surface with the underwater structure, creating a logical transition for the circulation of visitors and the distribution of spaces, as well as allowing for the constant expansion of the facilities—in exactly the same way as coral structures.

Egg

Marsupial

Temporary Animal Structures

Reproduction is a function common to all known forms of life. In the animal world, an embryo must be protected (once fertilization has occurred, whether internally or externally) until it reaches a certain state of development. Some animals are viviparous (from the Latin *vivus*, "alive," and *parire*, "to give birth"), including the majority of mammals, whose embryos grow in the mother's womb, where they receive everything required to form their organs, grow, and mature until they are ready to be born. Others are oviparous (from the Latin *ovum*, "egg," and *parire*, "to give birth"), and their reproduction process involves laying eggs in an external medium, where they complete their development before hatching.

A bird's egg is a capsule enclosed by calcareous walls, and its ellipsoid form, with a more obtuse curve at one end than at the other, endows it with great resistance. The walls of this sheath are porous, allowing gases to pass through it from both inside and outside. The embryo is inside, along with the nutritional tissues known as the yolk and white. A strong elastic membrane covers all these substances, which are attached to the walls of the egg by strands known as chalazae. The most obtuse part of the egg contains an air chamber or space that is essential to the breathing requirements of the young animal growing inside.

Apart from birds, the oviparous animals include most insects, fish, amphibians, reptiles, echidnas, and the platypus. Their eggs come in an astonishing range of shapes and sizes. Newly fertilized frogs, for example, search for a leaf on which they can hang a gelatinous mass containing up to a hundred eggs. In contrast, spiders wrap their eggs in silk, while butterflies' eggs are so small that they are only visible under a microscope, although their surface structure is enormously complex.

There is a halfway house between viviparous and oviparous animals—the marsupials. Unlike viviparous animals, marsupials do not produce a placenta, and this deficiency means that the fetus is born in a very premature state and must continue to grow in a pouch (or *marsupium*). This is formed from a crease in the abdominal skin and is closed by means of a mouth (marsupial sphincter) that isolates it from the exterior, providing greater security for the offspring. The pouch con-

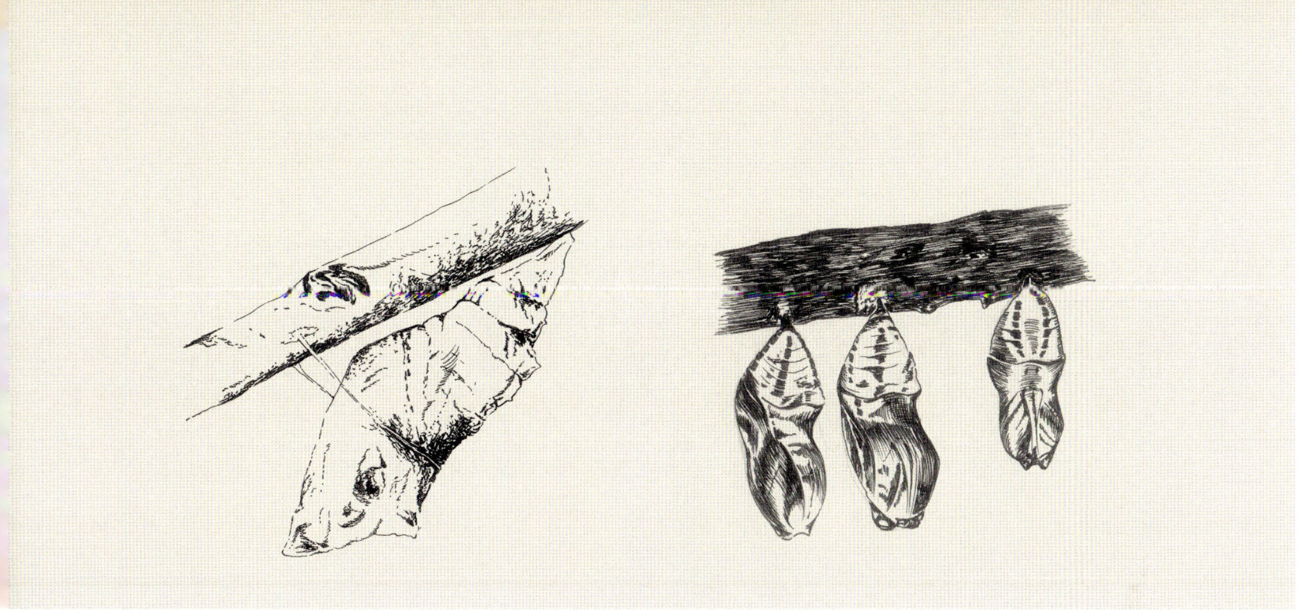

Pupa and Chrysalis

tains nipples that are connected to the mammary glands and reach the new embryo's esophagus.

Once the embryo has developed, whether in the egg, uterus, or marsupium, the new individual is incorporated into the life of its species. Some animals, such as mammals, change gradually until they become adults, and the main difference between the latter and the young is basically their size. In contrast, other species experience a metamorphosis, either complete or simple. A complete metamorphosis is an extremely complex process. An egg hatches a larva, which feeds voraciously, moves on to become a pupa—when it stops eating and usually remains immobile—and then wraps itself in a protective cocoon and undergoes a morphological and physiological reorganization that culminates in the formation of the adult insect or imago. This type of metamorphosis occurs in almost 80 percent of insects, as well as in some crustaceans.

The pupa is the state through which some insects pass from the larval stage to full adulthood. Unlike the latter two, the pupa stage is sessile, and during it the insect hides or encloses itself in a capsule to protect itself while the juvenile organs are absorbed and the organism adopts a totally different structure. In this stage, the insect is motionless and does not eat at all. It gradually grows legs and wings, which were not present in the larva, and its body takes on the characteristic three-part structure of head, thorax, and abdomen. The process can come to a climax in barely a couple of weeks, as in the case of some butterflies, or it can function as a rest period, in wait for favorable environmental conditions.

The pupa of butterflies and moths is known as a chrysalis (from the Greek *chrysos*, "gold"), and this is one of the most visually striking forms adopted by pupae. Most butterflies' chrysales are suspended throughout this process from a silky peduncle produced by the caterpillar and hidden in foliage for protection. Moths' chrysales, in contrast, are usually dark and are buried in the ground or wrapped in a cocoon. The silkworm's cocoon is particularly famous, thanks to the extremely long thread with which it is made. When the adult insect hatches, it breaks open the cocoon or dissolves it by excreting a liquid.

Marsupial

This house is situated in the residential neighborhood of Minato, one of the most densely populated districts of Tokyo, with approximately 22,344 people per square mile (8,627 people per square km^2) in 2005. This situation has given rise to buildings with very limited floor areas, particularly in the residential sector, where efforts are made to take full advantage of every possible inhabitable space. The architects took on the challenge of designing a home for a young family in the face of severe spatial restrictions—a surface area of only 431 square feet (40 m^2) and limited natural light, on account of the house's placement on the north side of the street in the shadow of the buildings opposite. The clients, a Japanese couple with two children, wanted a bright house adapted to the small dimensions, while being reasonably safe for the youngsters when their parents were not at home. In order to achieve luminosity and make the most of the confined space, the architects paid particular attention to the four main walls, especially the façade. The central part of the main façade is a swelling in the wall, inspired by the pouch of marsupials that gives them additional space in which they can feed their young. In this way, the living room also acquired an extra space, an architectural pouch extending from the interior to serve various functions, especially for the children. The SH House is now considered a model of architectural versatility and ingenuity, despite its logical, formal simplicity.

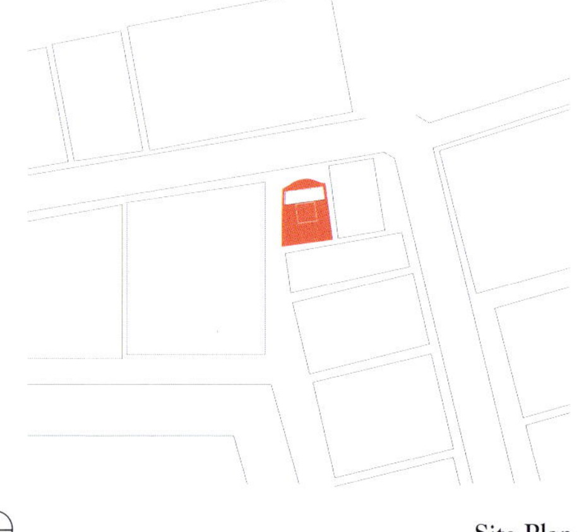
Site Plan

Client
Private

Type of Project
Family house

Location
Minato, Tokyo, Japan

Total Surface Area
431 square feet (40 m^2)

Completion Date
2005

Photos ©
Daici Ano, NAP Architects

Minato, Tokyo, Japan

SH House

Hiroshi Nakamura & NAP Architects

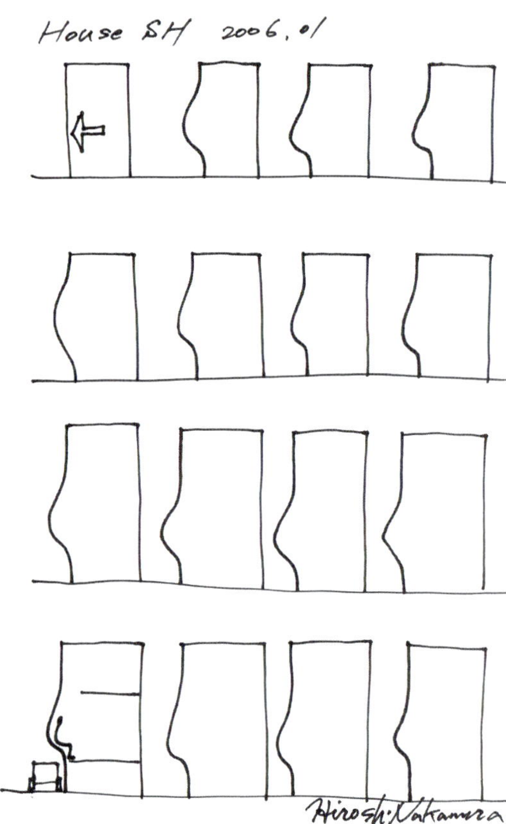

Preliminary Sketches

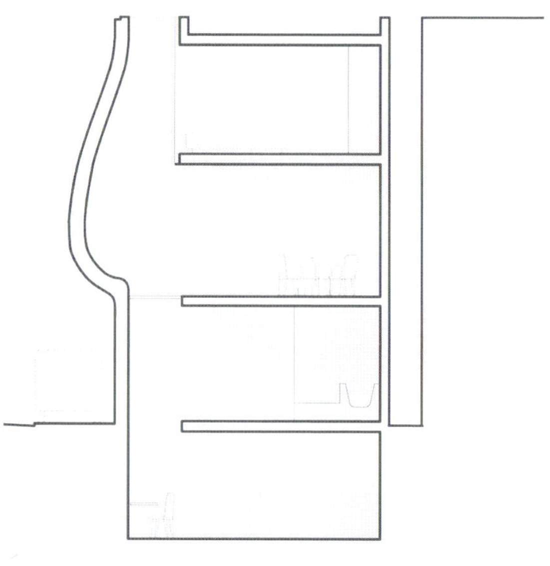

Cross Section

The design strategy grew out of a volume that occupies the small lot in its entirety, built on three levels set above an underground area reserved for parking. The next step was the creation of the central cavity or marsupium in the façade, which extends right to the outer limits of the perimeter of the house. The interior space was turned into a striking recess with rounded corners, which increases the effective dimensions of the living room by adapting to the needs of its inhabitants and providing a bench or couch. The problem of lighting was solved by means of a large skylight set in the roof of the marsupium, which enables natural light to enter and transforms the pouch into a light well running down to the ground floor of the house. The white wall efficiently reflects the light pouring in from the skylight, illuminating the spaces on every story and unifying the interior.

While the pouch, or marsupium, is the compositional element that unifies and characterizes the project, the staircase acts as its functional and sculptural axis.

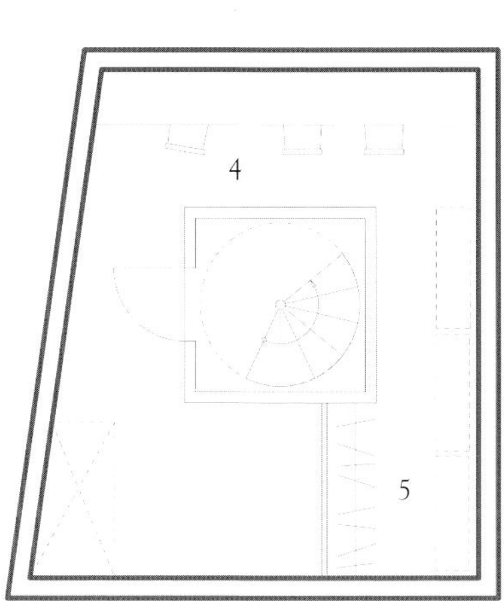

Plan of the Basement

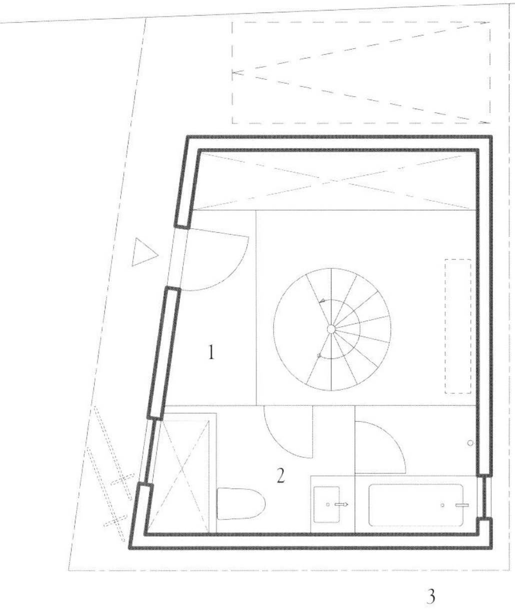

First Floor

1- Entrance
2- Toilet
3- Bathroom
4- Studio
5- Closet
6- Dining Room
7- Kitchen
8- Bedrooms

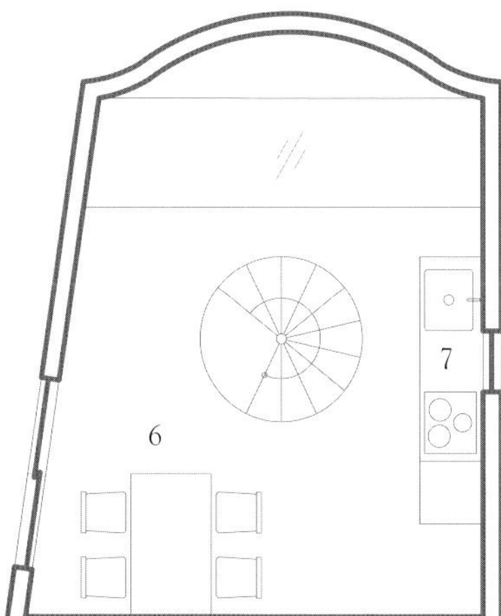

Second Floor

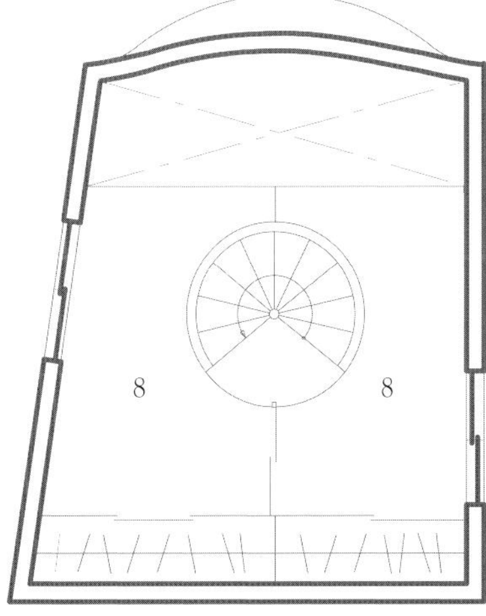

Third Floor

The house was built of concrete and painted white all over, to maximize the reflection of sunlight. Each floor corresponds to a distinct area in the house, so the kitchen, living room, bathroom, and bedrooms each occupy a whole story, linked by a spiral staircase running from the ground floor to the third level. The wall in the form of a marsupium, which is the unifying element in the house, also adds a humorous touch and offers the inhabitants the possibility of communicating to each other and making creative use of this resource in a host of different ways.

Pupa

This project is a raised pedestrian walkway connecting two parts of the Plashet School in Newham, London. It has come to be considered a highly original steel sculpture and has grown into an icon for the local community. The architects sought to create a dynamic structure that would not only serve to guarantee the safe passage of the teachers and pupils constantly crossing from one building to the other but also to protect them from inclement weather. The bridge thus was seen as both a shelter and a link, and accordingly the architects found inspiration in the strategy of caddis-fly larvae to assemble various construction materials. The bridge's light structural system passes over a busy road and alleviates the traffic problems that formerly arose during school hours. The use of steel and translucent Teflon protects pedestrians against rain while also allowing natural light to penetrate inside. The gallery in the middle of the walkway offers teachers and pupils a meeting place with views of the landscape. The bridge's sinuous geometry echoes the position of the trees that had grown up nearby. The project was conceived as an exercise in sustainable design, manifested in a piece of architecture that has given the school a new, more unified identity.

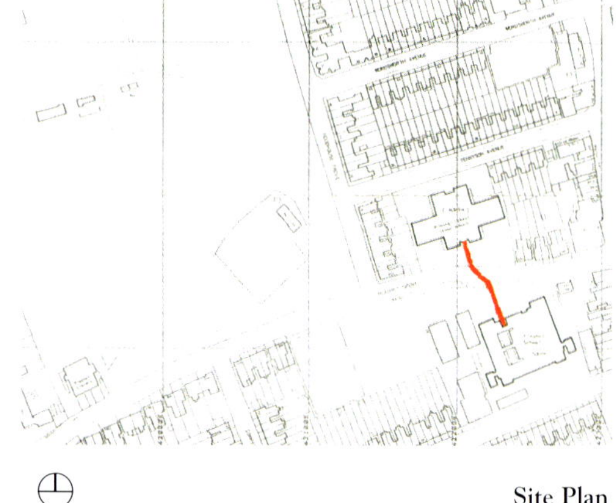

Site Plan

Client

Newham Council

Type of Project

Pedestrian bridge

Location

Newham, London, England

Length

220 feet (67 m)

Completion Date

2000

Photos ©

Birds Portchmouth Russum Architects, Nick Kane

Newham, London, England

Plashet Bridge

Birds Portchmouth Russum Architects

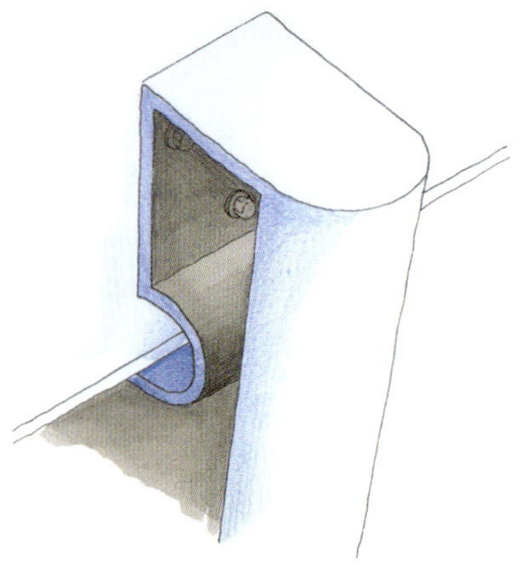

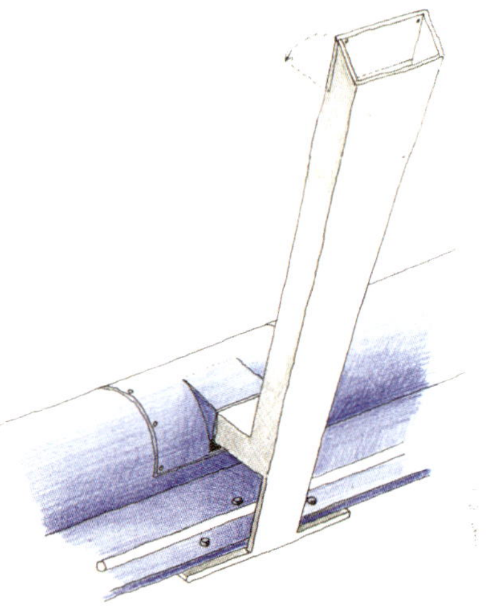

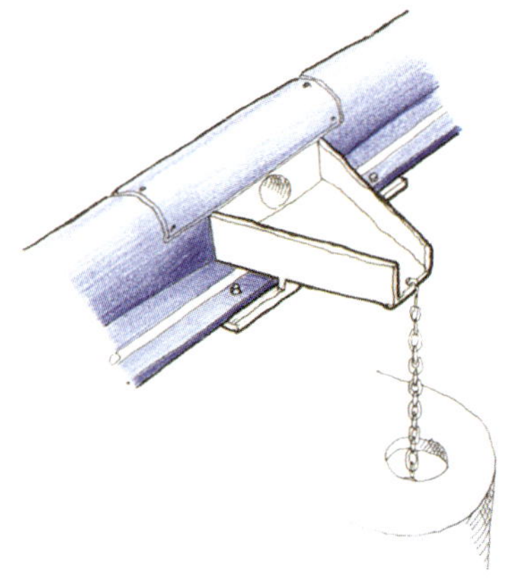

Studies of the Structure and the Clamps

The bridge is supported by steel columns rooted in a series of galvanized steel rings and covered with light Teflon. The structure's skeleton is divided into three sections and is soldered with steel beams 36 inches (915 mm) wide, topped by circular beams that round off the balustrade. The asymmetric rings alternate along the entire length of the structure, both consolidating it and giving form to the roof. Both ends of the bridge are held up by smaller columns that separate in the form of an inverted V, one of which acts as the northern entrance to the school. The bridge lies on two central beams, supported by several hollow clamps marking the form of the outer cladding, like a protective skin joining the two buildings together.

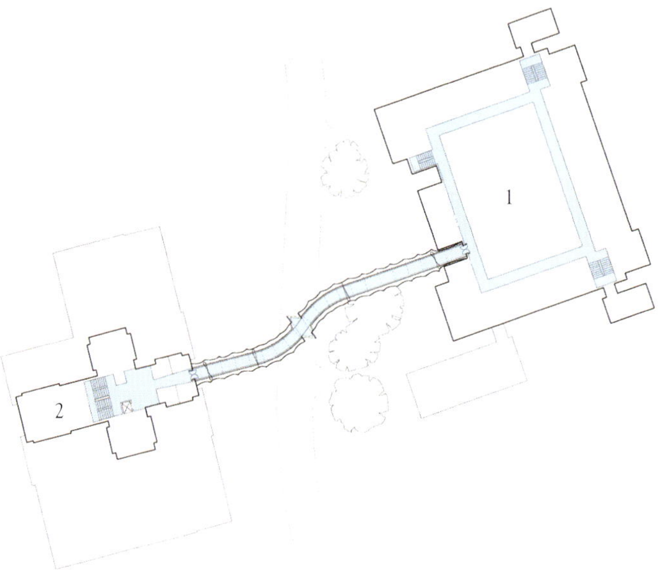

General Plan

1- North Building
2- South Building

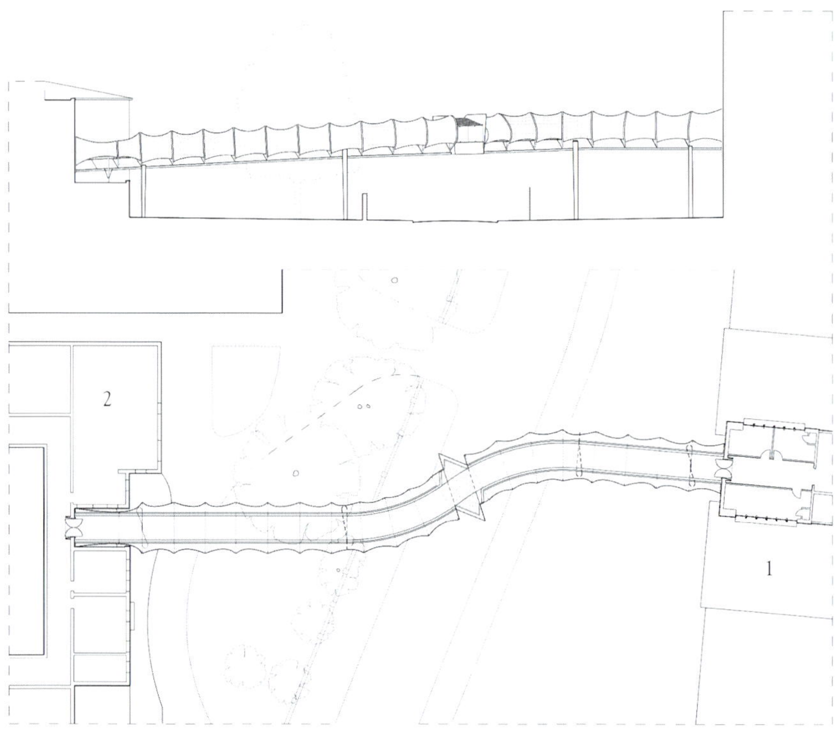

Elevation and Plan of the Walkway

The analogy of the larva in metamorphosis is evidenced by the very form of the structure, as by well as its elastic cladding material, which heightens the similarity with a pupa. This focus on physical growth and transformation is highly appropriate to a school.

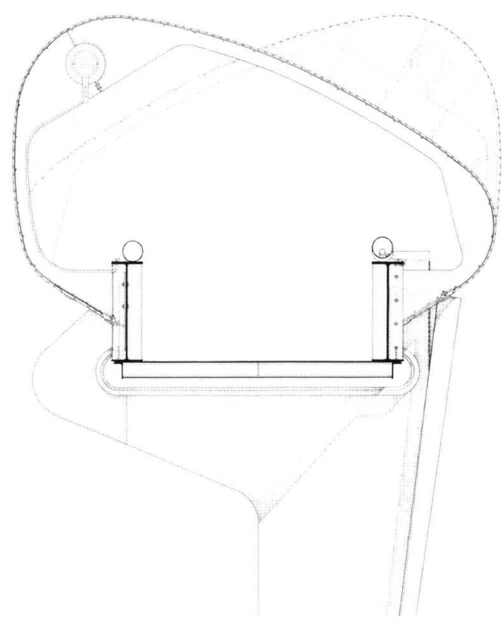

Cross Section

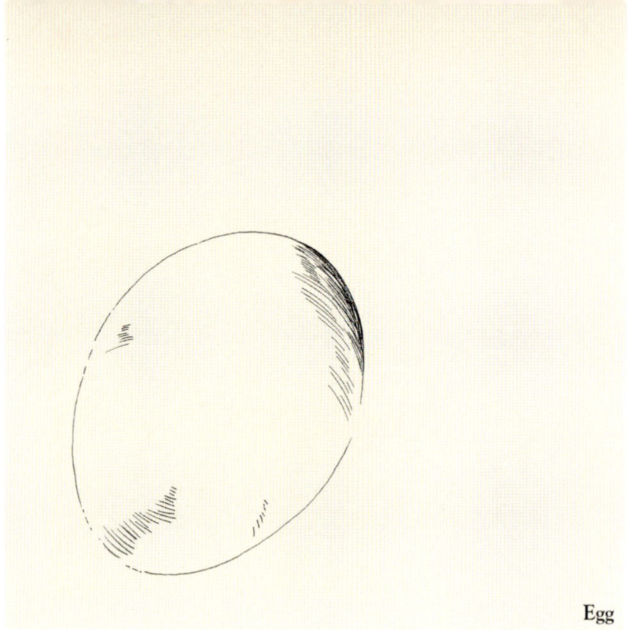

Egg

This revolutionary project was unveiled in 2005 as part of an exhibition in the Nagoya Concrete Art Museum, and it has taken concrete microtechnology to levels unheard of even in Japan. The concrete casing was conceived as a multifunctional structure suited to various situations. Its secret lies in the combination of materials used for its construction, as glass fiber has been integrated into the thin concrete. Inspired by the strategy of the cocoon, a portable refuge, and by the egg, thin but resistant, the multipurpose pod is a mere .6 inch (15 mm) thick and 5.6 feet (1.7 m) high—a ratio comparable to the proportions of a chicken's egg. Despite its lightness, the structure can support the weight of an adult on its tip. The pod can immediately be transformed by the addition of tatamis to become a quiet niche for relaxation or play. When transposed to a natural setting like a wood, the pod turns into another kind of space, as natural light can pour through its openings and the surroundings acquire a new lyrical intensity. The project was universally admired as an ingenious design concept and has won architecture awards all over the world.

Client

Nagoya Concrete Art Museum

Type of Project

Microspatial furnishing/temporary pavilion

Location

Nagoya, Japan

Total Surface Area

24 square feet (2.24 m^2)

Completion Date

2005

Photos ©

Ichiro Sugioka

Nagoya, Japan

Concrete Pod

Kazauya Morita Architecture Studio

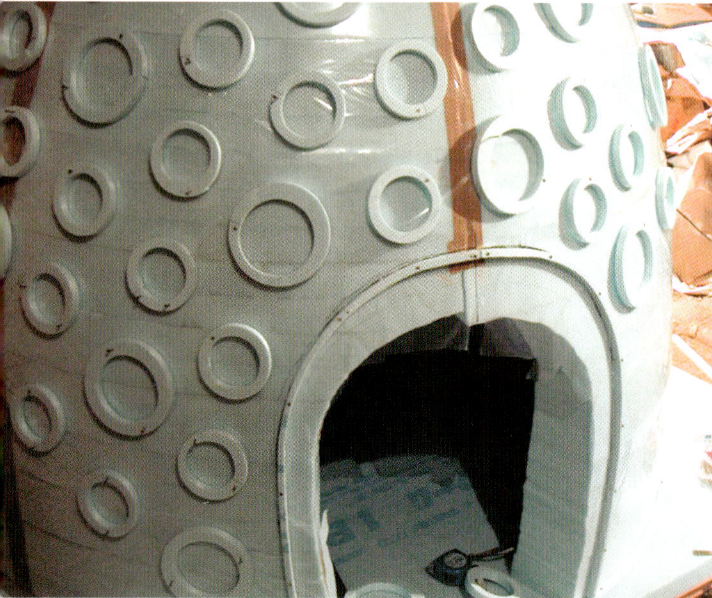

General Elevations

The structure's concrete cladding is reinforced by a substance that combines white cement, lightweight aggregate, and glass fiber. This mass is first carefully mixed and then spread with a spatula over a concave mold made of polystyrene foam, along the lines of the traditional Japanese plastering technique known as *sakan*. The perforations in the sides are achieved by embedding polystyrene rings all over the surface of the structure. Once the mass has hardened, it is turned out of the polystyrene mold. The result is a structure of great beauty, resistance, and simplicity.

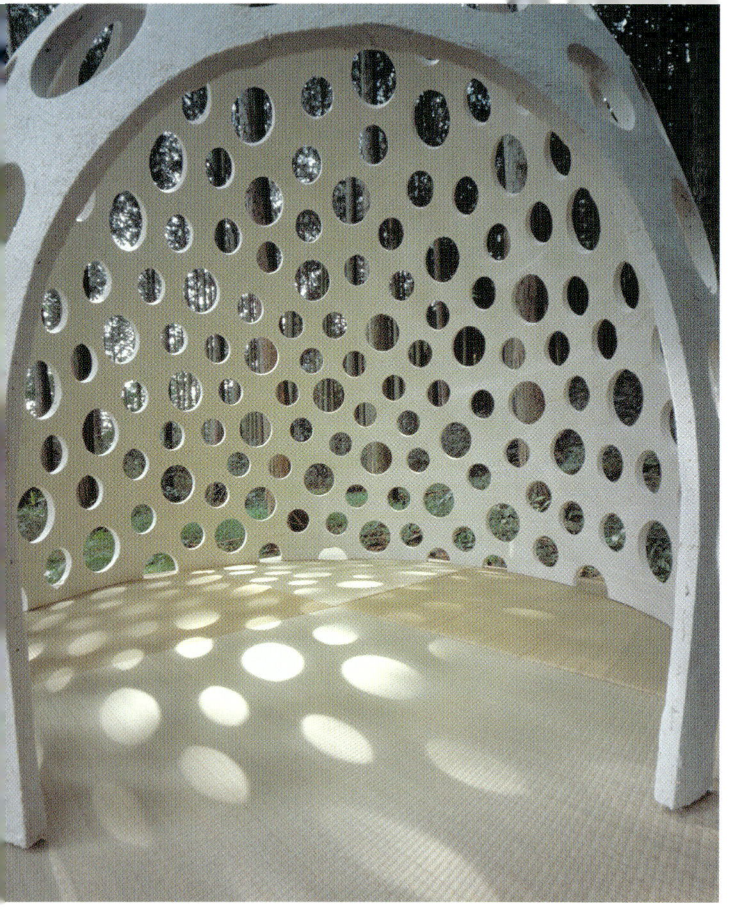

Thanks to the large number of openings dotting the structure, the exterior setting can still be appreciated from inside the concrete pod. Even the most fleeting visitor to this portable shelter may be carried away by a moment of deep relaxation and security, in an experience recalling the traditional tea ceremony or *cha-shitsu*. The traditional tatami floor contrasts with the sophisticated concrete pod set on top of it, combining two languages that reoccur in traditional Japanese architecture.

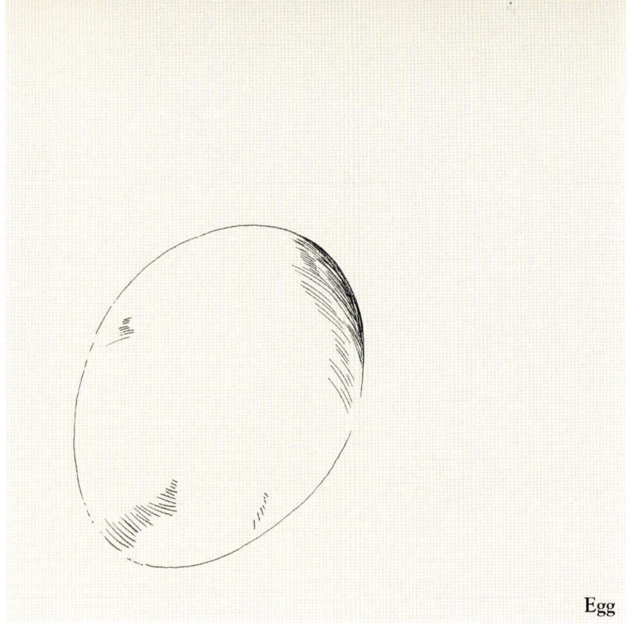

Egg

The Free University of Berlin has played a central role in the city's intellectual life since World War II, as its opening marked the rebirth of liberal education, and it went on to become one of Berlin's most emblematic institutions in this field. Today the university has over 39,000 students, making it one of the biggest in the city. The architectural evolution of the university has encompassed the restoration of modernist buildings and the redesigning of a new campus for the library. Two large elements stand out from the modernist era: the campus, designed by Candilis, Josic, Woods, Schiedhelm, and now considered a landmark of 1970s architecture; and the library façade, built by those architects in collaboration with Jean Prouvé and inspired by Le Corbusier's system of proportional modules. The steel used to shroud the library like a protective egg incorporated corrosive products that caused a swift deterioration of its exterior. So, the architectural team responsible for the building's refurbishment replaced the old steel with a new bronze cladding that would take on both the details and the color of the original material with the passing of time. The new library in the philology department occupies a space equivalent to the sum of six of the university's courtyards. The library's oval shape has earned it the nickname of "the Brain of Berlin."

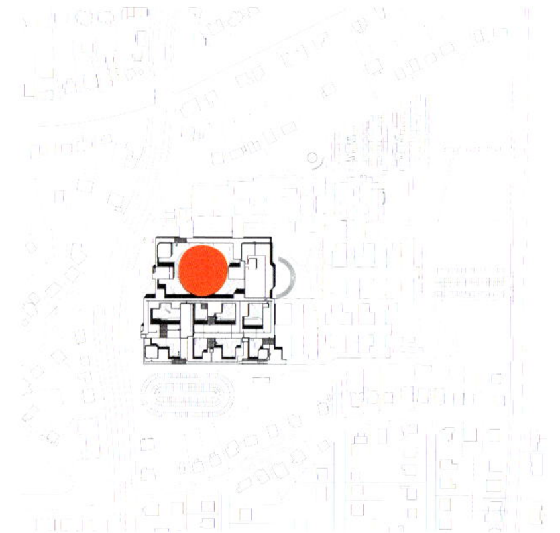

Site Plan

Client

Free University of Berlin

Type of Project

Library

Location

Berlin, Germany

Total Surface Area

497,293 square feet (46,200 m^2)

Completion Date

2004

Photos ©

Nigel Young, Reinhard Görner, Rudi Meisel

Berlin, Germany

Free University of Berlin

Foster + Partners

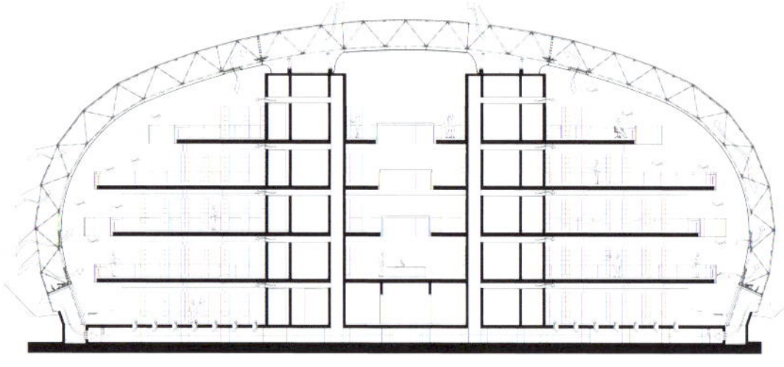

Cross Section

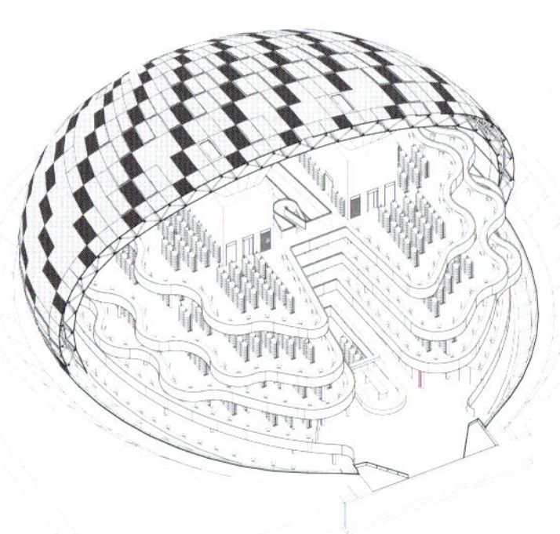

Sectioned Axonometric View

The four stories open to the public include a chamber in the form of a naturally ventilated bubble that is clad in aluminum, complemented by glass panels in steel frames arranged in a radial formation. An internal membrane made of translucent glass fiber filters the sunlight and creates an atmosphere of serenity and concentration, while some isolated openings offer glimpses of the sky. The bookshelves are set in the center of each floor, and the reading desks are distributed around the perimeter. The wavy outlines around the stories establish a pattern that fluctuates inward or outward with respect to the previous floor, thereby opening up light wells between each floor that are ideal workspaces.

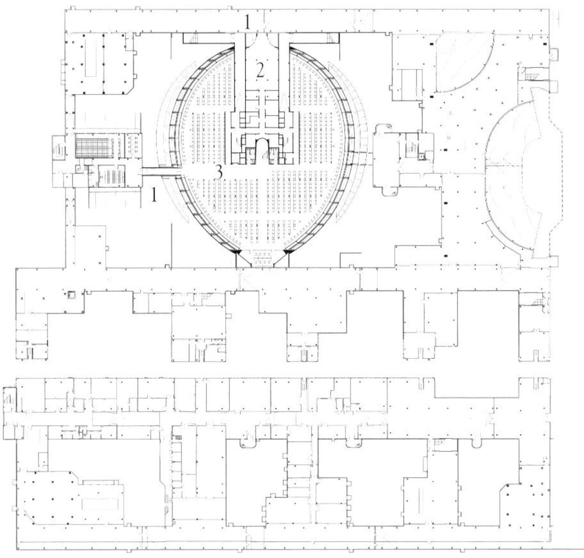

Ground Floor

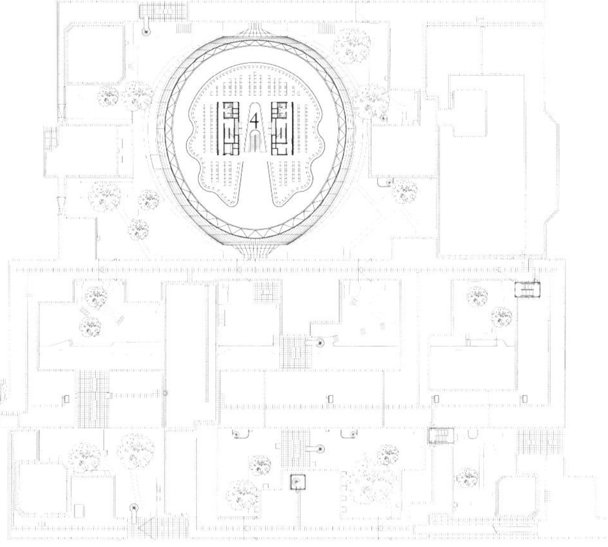

Second Floor

1- Entrance
2- Main Foyer
3- General Archives
4- Reading Room

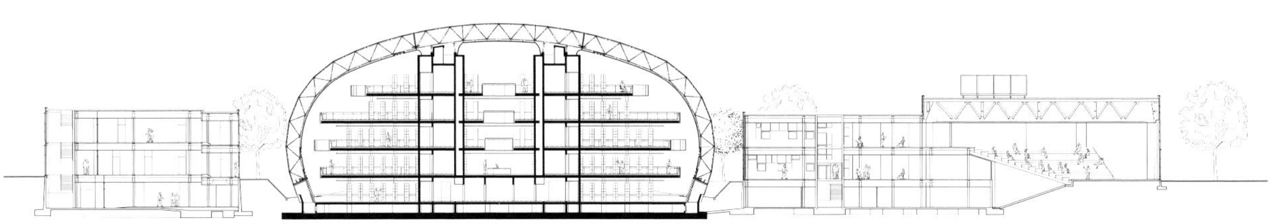

General Longitudinal Section

The library is a concrete structure divided into two large central areas. When the old façade was replaced by new bronze cladding, the main building was slightly altered to satisfy modern technical requirements. This process included the extraction of 211,888 cubic feet (6,000 m^3) of contaminated asbestos that formerly insulated the building. The roof was endowed with a zone of extensive vegetation that retains heat and also reduces the surface area of the second floor. The library, spread over five levels, boasts some 700,000 books and 36 reading rooms; it has successfully integrated other institutes and libraries that were formerly dispersed all over the city.

Index of Architects

Acconci Studio
20 Jay Street, Suite 215, Brooklyn, NY 11201
T: 1 718 852 6591
F: 1 718 624 3178
studio@acconci.com
www.acconci.com

Birds Portchmouth Russum Architects
Unit 11, Union Wharf, 23 Wenlock Road, London N1 7SB, UK
T: +44 020 7253 8205
F: +44 020 7253 5285
info@birdsportchmouthrussum.com
www.birdsportchmouthrussum.com

bube architects
Looiershof 29, 3024 CZ Rotterdam, The Netherlands
T: +31 06 4175 5685
info@bube-arch.net
www.bube-arch.net

Building Design Partnership
15 Exchange Place, Glasgow G1 3AN, UK
T: +44 0141 227 7900
F: +44 0141 227 7901
cc-allan@bdp.co.uk
www.bdp.co.uk

Damian Figueras
Cavallers 34, 08034 Barcelona, Spain
T: +34 606 088 028/44 794 4025 331
damianfigueras@hotmail.com

Eric Owen Moss Architects
8557 Higuera Street, Culver City, CA 90232
T: 1 310 839 1199
F: 1 310 839 7922
jose@ericowenmoss.com
www.ericowenmoss.com

fnp architekten
Heilbronnerstrasse 39a, 70191 Stuttgart, Germany
T: +49 0711 305 8006
F: +49 0711 305 8013
info@fischer-naumann.de
www.fischer-naumann.de

Foster + Partners
Riverside, 22 Hester Road, London SW11 4AN, UK
T: +44 020 7738 0455
F: +44 020 7738 1107
enquiries@fosterandpartners.com
www.fosterandpartners.com

Freie Architekten
Bismarckstrasse 15, D-64293 Darmstadt, Germany
T: +49 061 512 8805
F: +49 061 512 8806
kabux@t-online.de
www.kabux.de

Hiroshi Nakamura & NAP Architects
Sky Heights 3-1-9-5F, Tamagawa Setagaya-ku
Tokyo 158-0094, Japan
T: +81 03 3709 7936
F: +81 03 3709 7963
nakamura@nakam.info
www.nakam.info

José Gigante
Rua D. António Barroso 289, 4050-060 Porto, Portugal
T: +351 226 063 566
F: +351 226 094 044
joségigante@sapo.pt

Justo García Rubio
Obispo Segura Sáez, 15 - 4ºB, 10001 Cáceres, Spain
T/F: +34 927 241 205
estudiocaceres@justogarcia.com
www.justogarcia.com

Kazuya Morita Architecture Studio
4-6-2F-16 Kaguraoka-cho, Yoshida, Sakyo-ku, Kyoto 606-8311, Japan
T/F: +81 75 752 4333
moritakazuya@nifty.com
www.morita-arch.com

Marlon Blackwell
100 West Center Street, Suite 001, Fayetteville, AK 72701
T: 1 479 973 9121
F: 1 479 251 8281
info@marlonblackwell.com
www.marlonblackwell.com

matti ragaz hitz architekten
Schwarzenburgstrasse 200, CH-3097 Liebefeld-Bern, Switzerland
T: +41 031 970 0066
F: +41 031 972 0605
toni.matti@mrh.ch
www.mrh.ch

mmw architects
Schweigaardsgt.34d, n-0191 Oslo, Norway
T: +47 2217 3440
F: +47 2217 3441
mail@mmw.no
www.mmw.no

MONK architecten
Van Asch van Wijckskade 31, 3512 VR Utrecht, The Netherlands
T: +31 030 230 4227
F: +31 030 231 8606
monk@monk.nl
www.monk.nl

OFIS arhitekti
Kongresni TRG 3, 1000 Ljubljana, Slovenia
T: +386 1 426 0084-5
F: +386 1 426 0085
info@ofis-a.si
www.ofis-a.si

Petr Parolek
Soukopova 3, Brno 602 00, Czech Republic
T: +42 54 924 6363
parolek@volny.cz
www.parolli.cz

ppag architects
Gumpendorferstrasse 65/1, A-1060 Vienna, Austria
T: +43 01 5874 4710
F: +43 01 5874 4799
ppag@ppag.at
www.ppag.at

SAMI.arquitectos
Rua Augusto Cardoso, 58-2º, 2900-255 Setúbal, Portugal
T: +351 265 000 247
F: +351 265 000 315
info@sami-architects.com
www.sami-arquitectos.com

Toyo Ito & Associates, Architects
Fujiya Building 1-19-4, Shibuya Shibuya-ku, Tokyo 150-0002, Japan
T: +81 03 3409 5822
F: +81 03 3409 5969
kinoshita@toyo-ito.co.jp
www.toyo-ito.co.jp

UNStudio
Stadhouderskade 113, P.O. Box 75381, 1070 AJ Amsterdam, The Netherlands
T: +31 020 570 2040
F: +31 020 570 2041
info@unstudio.com
www.unstudio.com

Wilkinson Eyre Architects
24 Britton Street, London EC1M 5UA, UK
T: +44 020 7608 7900
F: +44 020 7608 7901
info@wilkinsoneyre.com
www.wilkinsoneyre.com